# Fuck the State!

By Harry Felker

# Table Of Contents

# Foreword

"Our integrity sells for so little, but it is all we really have. It is the very last inch of us, but within that inch, we are free."
~ V for Vendetta

*It was winter, when the night comes down early and the heavy snow hardens the surrounding dark. As soon as the school ended, I prepared myself for the long awaiting of the bus. It came, as usual, way too full of people pushing one another, each hoping to find a better place inside. Maybe I just stand on the stairs while it was rolling through the cold, like I did a lot of times. I don't remember. What I do remember, as vivid as it happened yesterday, is walking down the alley from the bus station to the building where I was living; in the dark, as, of course, it was during the "saving hours" so the electricity was cut. I didn't really care about this, I was following the whiteness of the snow, listening to the cotton sound of my footsteps while they printed their trace. Once in the building, I climbed quickly the seven floors, the elevator being stuck where the daily cutting caught it. Dark and dark again. But it still didn't matter, that night was my mother's birthday and I was eager to hold her in my arms. I opened the door of the apartment and stared at the only light of the candles. No, not the ones on the cake. My mother was still shaping it, tears running on her cheeks, liquefying the whipped cream. Suddenly the cold inside the kitchen sneaked inside my bones and struck all of my brain cells: rationalizations, restrictions, rules, a suffocating rhythm tightening progressively, grinning with vicious teeth. Unconsciously, my will wrote with fire the words to fight back: refuse, resist, rebel: I became an Anarchist.*

The frame of an individual's personality takes shape in his child's years. The way he perceives the world around him will determine his reactions through his thinking, more or less consciously, building what will be filled in the following years with knowledge, experience and understanding.

If we were to explore the individual's inward we might discover that the mechanism of thinking – *cogitare* meaning pondering as well - encompasses self control through a complex self delimitation between rights and wrongs. Then what happens when the concept of freedom guides an individual? Or, to be more precise, what is the logical culminant when one considers freedom in all its aspects, when it becomes a state of the being? The answer is: Anarchy, the very contestated label.

How can this be, one might ask...

Let us travel inside the word Eleutheria, which is the term for freedom in ancient and modern Greek. We will discover that it has two roots, *eleu* and *eran*. The root *eleu* has an understanding of "arriving" while *eran* means "love" with its declination *eria*, "one loves". So when we analyze these notions together we can say that one loves when arriving to the destination freedom. Exploring further on we can extrapolate this idea and comfortably affirm that when the individual, through his inner thinking – pondering and consideration - reaches the stage of freedom, then there is fulfillment of his love. And this is why freedom is a state of the being, as what can be more exclusive and self absorbing than love... Love elevates the individual to a higher level of consciousness and creates a dependence, or addiction, and when it expresses itself within the awareness of freedom then it naturally flows towards the abhorrence of any kind of rulers other than the individual himself.

The absence of rulers, freedom unrestricted by manmade laws, is the core meaning of the anarchist philosophy, which considers the Individual and his interactions with other Individuals and not the Society per se. The economic liberty releases human energy and the natural negotiation and cooperation between individuals has an anarchic quality and recognition of "mine" and "thine".

Thus the overall flourishment of human kind lays upon the two intrinsically related notions of freedom and anarchy.

"Anarchy means 'without leaders', not 'without order'. With anarchy comes an age or *ordnung*, of true order, which is to say **voluntary** order... this age of *ordung* will begin when the mad and incoherent cycle of *verwirrung* that these bulletins reveal has run its course." ~ V for Vendetta

Mr. Harry Felker's book is interesting at many levels. The one which touches me most is his mind's journey through the freedom land until he seized the shores of anarchism. Pragmatic, yet addicted to his love for freedom, he then started to build the knowledge within the pondering. He is sharing a part of it with you, so please enjoy the reading.

I love you baby....

# Preface

This book is a compilation of my work over the course of a couple years, adjusted for a consistent theme, the end of my support of limited government, or minarchism, in favor of total anarchism under a capitalist system of property ownership. I know full well that there are assumptions made at the earlier works that contradict the latter, this is quite honestly the case as I grew from supporting a limited system to no system of government at all.

Circa mid-2007 I had changed, from someone who was one of those "Deaf-Mutes" to someone who was beginning to become quite aware of the reality of the situation around me. Like most, barely aware something was wrong, but not caring enough to really think about it; maybe I was too busy just surviving to notice. Then someone had thrown it in my face, that someone was Dr. Ron Paul, there was something direly wrong with the America I live in. I began to take notice. I looked at the world and really paid attention and it was inescapable, verily inconceivable that I did not notice this beforehand; I would say I was dumbfounded, but I was far too angry at the state of affairs. I had written a couple of poetry pieces that summer in reflection of my awakening to the inherent wrongness I felt but still was not aptly equipped to identify.

For a year after I had been studying, reading and commenting on social interaction sites and forums in order to really understand what was wrong with what I had come to know as the US and what it ought to be. I had sought council in the Declaration of Independence, The Constitution, and other historical sources, all the time commenting on what it was I was finding and what it meant in reference to the current state of affairs.

I had eaten the pill of Ron Paul's limited government doctrine; the support seemed to be there from the founding documents, that a government ought to be limited in power to protect its citizen's liberties. In this respect I do have a sense of gratitude to Ron Paul, without his presidential bid I may have been scrolling around in the dark for much longer. I had believed that government had a proper role, to defend the liberty of its citizens, the three branches defended the citizens from each other and in the worst case the citizens had the obligation to be the last line of defense for their liberty.

I knew the problem was the government and I believed that it was the monolithic and out of control nature it displayed, I was literally grabbing at all straws for a solution. I knew the people I needed to get the attention of were diverse and unwilling to use the certain tactics; I could not convince a pacifist to fight just as I could not convince a militarist to hunger strike. I began to grow and develop an underlying theme, the morality of liberty, men ought to be free, and I began to understand more exactly what was wrong.

In the course of the 2008 election cycle, I had researched many parties, I was a republican in order to vote for Ron Paul in the primary, to no avail, after then though I was looking for a party that would do, or at least move in the direction I desired. I had looked into the "third" parties of the United States: Libertarian Party (LP), Constitution Party (CP) and The Boston Tea Party (BTP). Each of these had proposed the limited government I believed in, but after delving deeply into each yielded poor results at best. The LP had chosen Bob Barr who was what I refer to as a defected republican, meaning he was in favor of the large state; his acceptance to LP was based on his laissez faire attitude towards business. At this time I was unsure if it was Barr's sneakiness or the LP desire to gain power and capitalizing on other defected republicans. The CP was represented by Chuck Baldwin, and the CP had espoused a limited government doctrine, as Baldwin did himself, but they had a desire to impose religious law. Where the CP was in favor in word to limiting the power of government, they were not in favor of limiting it so much that it could not legislate their religious doctrine upon the people. The BTP was unfortunately not popular enough to have Charles Jay, their presidential candidate for the 2008 election, in more than 3 states and available for write-in in 10 other states. The BTP's main issue of being 2 years old and an abysmally low membership had a dire effect on their chances on making a serious bid for president; this also did not give me any assurance that they will do as they say once in an elected position.  In the end, I resigned to write-in Ron Paul, his congressional record was very indicative that he retained integrity in office, not that I was certain he would win this way, but rather as a symbol.

I had, after the election cycle, began writing in earnest, and this is the bulk for the collection here, I had joined forces, to turn a phrase, with many patriots of different walks of life, to spread the message of liberty beyond the election cycle.  Primarily to retain interest in the public at large, but also as a method to truly sort out my ideas into a solid format.

Granted, at the time I was challenged heavily, by those who aligned with the contemporary defined labels of conservative and liberal alike, each one accusing me of being the other.  My views on controversial topics such as gay marriage, abortion and war had given me the title of "ultra left wing moon-bat" by the religious right and other such sympathizers.  Conversely my views on markets, property/gun ownership and individual rights gained me the label of "neo-con capitalist exploiter" by the socialist left and their "comrades".  There really seemed to be no place for me, the internet communities for the most part were filled with ad hominem and straw-man tactics for debate, I was running out of room to grow.  I had also gained the label of Randian, or Randroid, because I had mentioned that I liked Ayn Rand's writings, that they were a good basis of thought in regard to the concepts of production, eudaimonia, individual liberty, money and such.  Though, it has been made apparent that because she did not think it was acceptable for the government to fleece business owners, she was her own variety of evil. This had always struck me when I read it, it was greedy for the business owner to want to keep his profits, but it was not greedy for the citizen to want to take them.  I had always thought that welfare was an impractical application of the state, but this argument had solidified a new direction for my disapproval of the welfare system, immorality.  The argument posed against me was created in envy, not by the destitute, they were not the ones populating the internet, but by middle class members. These people looked to the government to take from the richer than themselves, while leaving their own wealth undisturbed; I had adopted the principle of taxation as theft, seeing these middle class suburbanites objection toward lifting the tax burden from all.

---

I would be remiss that the latter portion of this book would not be possible without my wife, she has been an inspiration, and remains so today, and patiently waited for me to come to the logical conclusion of anarchism.

# Chapter I: Awakening

## Freedom

Land of the free, home of the brave.
We fool ourselves, each a lowly slave.
We all obey a hidden master.

Each of us, gripped ever faster.
False morality, codes of conduct.
Leads us on a path to self destruct.
They even attempt to control emotion.
We as people accept the notion.

We as people, desensitized.
By far too few have realized.
This is a prison within our mind.
More efficient than any kind.
They feed us prisoners their petty lies.
Bewildering the people before their eyes.
They keep us in line, mentally infected.
All the while they're never suspected.
Deviously declaring we all have a voice.
Lesser of two evils is still a bad choice.

People all fear my unquenchable hate.
I eternally refuse a sheepish slave's fate.
So few like me, few can understand.
Masquerading as free, yet submitting to demand.
We are forced to censor our actions and speech.
People need to learn this lesson I teach.
Freedom is not free, there is a heavy price.
Feelings will be hurt, free doesn't mean nice.

One should only speak with a true mind.
Pure honesty is all one should find.

In truth and honesty, we all should respect.
And treacherous deceit, no longer suspect.
I can only hope everyone understands.
Why I am so passionate in my demands.
I cannot believe freedom is a vice.
The feelings of the few is a paltry price.
All in this land, supposedly free.
Control blinds people so freedom we never see.

## National Anthem

(This was intended to be a song)

We are ruled by very few men
They fail the masses again and again
How long must we play their game
When they lose they just shift the blame

They're expected to lead, they treat us like fools
Constrict us with laws and break their own rules
We look to them and hope to survive
But on the backs of the masses these few thrive

Music Begins

Land of the free home of the brave
the rich are free while the poor are slaves
Land of the free home of the brave
the rich get to live and the poor get graves

I will not be led by a dollar sign
I will not obey, I am not that blind
I will not be led by a dollar sign
No one controls me, you're outta your mind

Land of the free home of the brave
the rich are free while the poor are slaves
Land of the free home of the brave
the rich get to live and the poor get graves

It's a crime to let this continue
Against all humanity
Our revolution on the horizon
Freedom is seldom free

Blood was spilled to create this freedom
Wasted on theocracy

Our streets must run red again
Freedom is seldom free

When dollar bills equal morality
morals are fake, don't you see.
When dollar bills make you free
Our time has come. Don't you see

# Chapter 2: Minarchism

## Attention, attention...

Ladies and Gentlemen, I wish to address you, those who support a government that does not work for you, those who are lying quietly while being raped...

A man tells you that you should put on these handcuffs, and climb in the back of his van, he promises nothing bad will happen, and that after a little while he will let you go, and he will offer you anything you want, aside from release, while you are cuffed.  But he does promise to let you go, after a little while...

A person is sitting in their van on the street corner, offering candy and gifts in his van to all passing children...

Why does this scenario make you think the people with handcuffs or candy are inherently evil, but when it is the government doing the same basic thing it is acceptable?

When the government says give up the right to bear arms, how are they not like the man with the handcuffs, how are they any better, how do they justify the people giving up the right to fight tyranny that would be sourced from them? They do it by telling you that they are our government and these things could never happen in the United States, they tell you that the government is here to help, that they love you, they are your big brother, in quite the Orwellian fashion. They expect you to believe that you must give up this one thing, your ability to fight back against them, in order for them to protect you from bad people. They expect you to believe that if you are stripped of the means to fight tyranny, these same means will vanish from the earth, and not even those who victimize law abiding citizens would have them. Only the government would have these means, and they love you, so they would never turn them on you, they love you so they would never oppress you, except of course if you view taking the right to bear arms away from individuals as oppression.

When they say give us your tax dollars (economic freedom) and we will offer you health care and cash assistance for free, how exactly is this different from the man with candy? They tell us it is for the greater good, that it is to help so many people, and they love all the people, after all we are one big national family, and everyone is their brother's keeper. They proclaim it is the burden of the rich to pay for the poor, and that individuals cannot be trusted to donate to charity, so the government must take it with guns and threats of prison, or in some cases, death. Every time they utter taxpayers they mean fuel, and every time they say government they mean inefficient machine, government in their eyes is a machine that eats a quarter of the lives of the average taxpaying citizen, for this fuel it puts out maybe 1% of the input as output, the other 99% is eaten by an inefficient machine. Taking candy from a stranger is a bad idea, why is it a good idea for the same mentality when it comes from your government, often, oddly enough, at your own expense?

## How do you represent having a line drawn?

There are four ways to draw your line, with your vote, with your voice, with your dollars and finally with your weapons, there are no other ways, all the rest is compliance. In the past decade, and even further if you are astute to this country's history, the vote is a failed tactic, you do not have to fool all the people all the time, just 3% more than the other major party candidate, and either way it does not matter as they are fighting the same war against we the people, the war for power. Next you can vocalize, but as Brozak said, "when you scream at the deaf, you just lose your voice," and there is no way to make those that must listen hear you, as their ears are full of ash, provided astutely by MSM, or are deliberately ignoring you, in the case of public servants. Tax protest, real protest, which is not paying you taxes on the individual basis is given the consequence of massive fines if not imprisonment, despite being what was supposed to be a completely voluntary program. The only way tax protest will work is if the entire state you reside in refuses to accept dollar one from, or remit dollar one to the federal government. I find this an eloquent plan that will most likely never pan out, because if the precedent is set with the federal government, the state may be subject to it next, and they would not like it too much. It is the idea that one should never make it possible to be shot with one's own gun that will keep this from happening, unless your state legislators are very short sighted. Lastly is violent revolt, a possibility that many are not too happy to consider, but in the sense of realism, even if every other route were possible, violence would always be the defining moment, whenever liberty is at stake, life will have to be lost, this is something Thomas Jefferson understood, and is quoted, "As our enemies have found we can reason like men, so now let us show them we can fight like men also."


So now, what is it, does slavery equal freedom, does freedom equal slavery or is it that freedom equals freedom and slavery equals slavery? There is a well known expression that freedom is not free, this is absolutely true, it comes from many sources but as to its meaning, it does not mean to send your children off to another country to fight and maybe die, it means that you may be inconvenienced in order to preserve the freedom that was offered by the authors of the Constitution. You may be inconvenienced, in order to repay the debt in blood that was paid at the end of the 18th century in order to preserve a nation founded on the principles of liberty and freedom for all. You may be inconvenienced; you may spill your blood to nourish the tree of liberty, forging the same blood debt on future generations to preserve the freedom for their future generations.

---

## Liberty, the Moral Choice.

For the premise of my commentary, I must first familiarize everyone that reads further with a quote from Ayn Rand, I am of the knowledge that some people do not like her, but this is the assumption on which the foundation of my commentary sits, and I fully believe this assumption to be true as it is not open to contradiction.

"Achievement of your happiness is the only moral purpose of your life, and that happiness, not pain or mindless self-indulgence, is the proof of your moral integrity, since it is the proof and the result of your loyalty to the achievement of your values."
~Ayn Rand[1]

As happiness is the moral purpose of your life, happiness is a prime value, not sacrifice, and not mindlessness this leads to the question of how one stands the best chance to achieve happiness. For the purpose of this proof we are going to examine liberty and its opposite, slavery, logically if I am to prove liberty is the moral choice I must examine slavery as a moral choice and be able to denounce it as false. Slavery offers no happiness, we do not achieve happiness at the sacrificial alter of the looting and mooching people demanding our best effort as their right offering nothing in return. Liberty requires our best effort, our best virtues, as liberty grants all the freedom of existence, but the responsibility to not take the existence

---

1

http://www.brainyquote.com/quotes/quotes/a/aynrand124862.html

from others.

Slavery as a moral choice was defended in the centuries past as the burden of those that have beset on them by their slaves, that the slave is merely a moocher that offers poor and forcefully provoked labor in return for the necessities of life. The slave sees that none of his effort is his own and he is the property of the whip holder, in current times slavery has changed in form but never in function. This is an important truth, slavery exists today as it had at this country's founding, instead of the slaves being brought in on ships from Africa, and they are born here, of all races and genders. The only marked difference in this is the hand holding the whip, for now it is the federal government, and it has been since 1865, it started then as a small snowflake sliding down the mountain, now we have a full blown avalanche on our hands. The illusion of freedom has been the subject matter of the public education system for some time, the declining quality in education, force-feeding the new American ideology on the students. Children are being manipulated to accept slavery, this is a key point to the amorality of slavery; if it cannot come natural to a child there is an issue with it, and our schools are demanding children to not question authority, to obey unflinchingly, as one would expect from a slave. One must then ask, is there happiness in this tactic for training the children, does the result produce happy individuals? If a teacher is happy producing a mindless drone, then they are the most evil creature ever to exist on Earth, the kind of sadist that enjoys with glee the handle of the lash as they strip away the minds of the future. There is no joy to be had in slavery, in any form of justification it is a burden, on both the slave and the master, each is forced to produce for the benefit for another, and never truly owns his own production. Slavery is therefore removed from the moral choice and into the realm of the amoral, as it achieves no happiness for any but the most depraved sadists, and it as an institution, past and present, has no value to humanity.

Liberty, in all beliefs that are true and just to humans, is the ideal, some are flawed in their methods, but they do all recognize the benefits of liberty. The religious believe that man is gifted life from a creator, and only reason dictates that if we are all children of a true and just "God" then one must accept, as we are his children, that this creator will want the best for us. What better opportunity than in liberty is presented to reach this goal, and in reaching the best for us, would that also dictate that there is happiness in the result? Atheists believe there is no such creator, and that life is the result of random action, does this deny that liberty is the best option? I would think not, as one's happiness is one's own responsibility, not having to answer to a "higher" being, the atheist should look to all opportunity to achieve happiness. Moral virtue is more than a religion can own, it is a value, and all value has a way to be exchanged, happiness as a moral value is exchanged only by volition. Take the example of the business owner and the employee, the business owner is made happy when his business thrives, and in order for this he requires the effort of men that are motivated to the task. The employer will, in true appreciation of value, reward the diligent and able worker, both are happy, the employer, as his business will prosper through better quality product from his employees, demanding a higher price for his product, and the employees, as they are finely rewarded in a just manner for their best efforts. This is directly opposite of slavery, slavery requires that someone must sacrifice value in order to provide for others, only in liberty can this scenario be made possible.

Logically, if happiness is a value to humanity, and to achieve one's values is a moral virtue, than choosing the best chance to achieve happiness must also be a moral choice. There is little argument that the end of a whip provides happiness, for either participant in the act, the whipped is obviously not in agreement, and the whipper is never pleased with the product. The only conclusion is that liberty is the only moral choice, further the only choice that will achieve any moral value, as any choice that is not liberty must be bought at the price of chains on someone, somewhere.

# Liberal vs. Conservative, the play on words to enslave a nation

In my experience many people like the label mentality, the belongingness to a collective, a group to share identity with; this is particularly evident in political ideologies, specifically the spectrum of liberal and conservative. I have a feeling that people have very subjective definitions for these terms, and this is the cause for a lot of contention, I think that a little adherence to the objective definitions would allow an individual to concretely define what people actually mean when they claim to be liberals or conservatives. I will attack definitions on multiple fronts, those being: political, social and financial, and how they take on a different meaning to the base concepts of liberal and conservative. I will also take on the contradiction in terms of the definition of Libertarianism, the socially liberal and fiscally conservative political philosophy in order to explain why the definition is right and those who like to use it are wrong.

## 1      The Objective vs. the Subjective

I find, in my experience in dealing with others, that a great many find one issue that they feel is important, seek out leaders that agree with it and assign themselves a label accordingly with their leader of choice.  Examples are evident everywhere around you, "liberals" espouse freedom of choice (abortion issue) as a liberty, but often balk at the idea that one has the right to defend oneself (2nd Amendment), conversely "conservatives" respect the freedom of self defense and armament (2nd Amendment), and reject the notion that an individual can put anything in their body that they choose (drug legislation).  These are examples of subjective definitions, a type of illogical conclusion that "I believe this and since my leader does as well, everything I believe is under this banner," is most prevalent with this misguided beginning.  Most often in the United States, the two parties system propagates this illusion, taking their extreme views to distract the populace from the base belief that the two parties share, large government.

Let's put to the test the objective definitions of conservatism and liberalism and see if we can have a consensus with the political dogma of partisan politics, or do we see a split from the objective and the subjective definitions of these terms.

Liberalism is defined as follows by Merriam-Webster [2]

1: the quality or state of being liberal

2 a: *often capitalized*: a movement in modern Protestantism emphasizing intellectual liberty and the spiritual and ethical content of Christianity b: a theory in economics emphasizing individual freedom from restraint and usually based on free competition, the self-regulating market, and the gold standard c: a political philosophy based on belief in progress, the essential goodness of the human race, and the autonomy of the individual and standing for the protection of political and civil liberties d (*capitalized*) : the principles and policies of a Liberal party

---

2 "Liberalism" Merriam-Webster Online Dictionary. 2009. Merrlam-Webster Online. 15 February 2009
http://www.merriam-webster.com/dictionary/liberalism

Conservatism is defined as follows by Merriam-Webster [3]

1 (*capitalized*) a: the principles and policies of a
Conservative party b: the Conservative party

2 a: disposition in politics to preserve what is established b:
a political philosophy based on tradition and social stability,
stressing established institutions, and preferring gradual
development to abrupt change; *specifically*: such a
philosophy calling for lower taxes, limited government
regulation of business and investing, a strong national
defense, and individual financial responsibility for personal
needs (as retirement income or health-care coverage)

3: the tendency to prefer an existing or traditional situation
to change

The current liberal notion in politics is one that favors a
political philosophy of progress and reform, entitlement

---

3 "Conservatism" <u>Merriam-Webster Online Dictionary</u>.
2009.  Merriam-Webster Online. 15 February 2009
<u>http://www.merriam-</u>
<u>webster.com/dictionary/conservatism</u>

spending, collective rights (women, blacks, gays), socialism (spreading the wealth) and curtailing individual rights for collective interests.  This is subjective, because as we can see in the objective definition the political philosophy does not match at all with the definition, as you cannot believe in the goodness of Human Beings and individual autonomy and have socialism and collective rights at the same time, they are indeed contradictory.  Even if you wish to focus on the progress part of the definition, one would think that liberals would seek changing the way things are, we are already wrought with socialism, and the liberal movement is to stay the course or even further the extent of this trend.  With the existence of socialist policy in the United States, liberals in this sense are more in alignment with conservative politics, "disposition in politics to preserve what is established".  In addition if we examine how the socialist policy has been increasing over the years, in a steady gradual pace, there is commonality with conservatism in this aspect, "preferring gradual development to abrupt change".

Following suit, the current conservative notion in politics makes claims to smaller government, less regulation and lower taxation in word, but in action conservative politicians expand federal power in the name of security and regulate individual rights just as avidly as "liberals".

This is subjective in word but objective in action, and probably is why many people distrust "conservative" politicians as a rule, where the "liberal" politicians are treated with more public trust.  How it is objective in action is as I revealed in the liberal discussion above (preferring gradual) and the final entry of the definition, "the tendency to prefer an existing or traditional situation to change". This is the specific place of contradiction with current "conservatism" as the current situation, the "existing" situation, is socialism, and gradually increasing socialism at that, I believe that the first entry is most applicable "disposition in politics to preserve what is established".  My constant question to those that are "conservative" is how can you advocate policing the world in the first sentence, and lower taxation and small federal government, for that matter how can one balance conservatism and constitutionalism where the Constitution does not allow for policing the world?

## 2      The Truth about Economic Liberalism

In truth there is no representation of economic liberalism as a party platform in major partisan politics, as this philosophy is quite against the concept of government intervention in the market place.  There is no instance in the Constitution that gives the government any right to participate in the market, aside from the purchaser of goods and services and "To regulate Commerce with foreign Nations, and among the several States, and with the Indian Tribes"[4].

Republicans make the claim for the free market, but in this instance they have a tendency to hedge out small business in regulations and fees in favor of large corporate interests, with very few exceptions. Democrats, the (very erroneously) self proclaimed liberal party, is far more hostile to economic liberalism, favoring economic planning and nationalization of private industry, this is a concept I like to call economic totalitarianism, as I feel it is far more appropriate to the system. No more debate can be made between the corporatists and communists as they both have in recent time used the exact same tactic for dealing with the exact same issue, of course I am speaking of the financial crisis of 2008-09. George Bush headed the stimulus package and corporate bail out, meanwhile less than a year later we have the same tactic used to stimulate the economy by nationalization, encouraged hiring (however unwise) and increased regulation.

Now to the other part of the definition, commodity based currency (the Gold Standard), we have very few and far between supporters of the only sound money the world has ever experienced, the Gold Standard. One would be hard pressed to find a supporter in major party politics that

4 US Constitution Article I Section 8

was taken seriously, and there is a good reason for this, the platforms of both major parties have accepted fiat currency, as this is the only means to their ends.  The commodity-based currency is by far the only liberal currency standard, it promotes individual liberty, taking the government printing press out of the equation, which only serves to rob the wealth of the people to afford the ever-expanding federal government.

## Socialism is anti-social

Given the name socialism by advocates in the early 19th century, is a set of principles that endorses "fairness" through the state in all matters, placing equality in the hands of state officials rather than the individuals.  There is a misnomer that socialism and communism is vastly different concepts, this is quite untrue, as the separation of these ideologies was made because of the similarity between the words communism and communion, and the prevailing socialist thought of the time was held by atheists.  Many people adhere that socialism is a fair way to deal with social aspects as it makes the state the constant arbiter of all aspects of life.  This notion leaves the true liberal with the thought that the state and those who advocate socialism are unable to handle liberty.  More so they are morally too weak to not indulge in the excesses that require state intervention to make certain that which they would do to their fellow man would not be redoubled on them.  Socialism is the condom of human interaction, keeping people from freely communicating and intermingling, keeps separate the marriage of ideas that can spring great invention.  Both political parties look for socialism as the ends to the means of their efforts, the increase of power to the level of total control of the individual.  Monetary policy is the poster boy of American socialism, this has made all other social aspects of our government possible, and quite expected gains the support of both major political parties, in the name of "there is no other way to survive."  The true liberal does not need the government to tell him how to talk, how to live and how to interact with others; he needs true and unbridled freedom, something socialism cannot supply.  The true liberal will give of his own will to charity and does not need the barrel of a gun in the hands of federal agents to be morally correct.  The true liberal never imposes his need on others by force, but rather appeals to reason, or will exchange value for value, the willingness to work for ones needs as opposed to having them granted based on his need.  The individual right to work is not necessary when the individual's right to achieve is present, without the hindrance of the federal monkey on his back forcing compliance with policy he does not agree with.

My analysis is that there are a left and a right conservative politics represented in the major parties, and I will admit that I wrongly labeled myself as conservative, having not fully researched as I have for this essay. Adherence to true liberal ideology, as the founders have in the creation of the Constitution, is not found in the political spectrum of today, at least with the major parties. I will now call a spade a spade; there are two conservative parties that should be justly called the Communist (Left/Democrat) Conservative Party and the Corporatist (Right/Republican) Conservative Party and in fact there is no Liberal party in major partisan politics. Constitutionalists should get used to this fact, that there is no party to conserve the Constitution in major politics, as this would be an objectively liberal party, furthermore, I would suggest that the constitutionalists abandon the label conservative and stop playing the game the major parties are playing. This terminology is used to make a collective that will justify non-Constitutional government policy in the name of keeping unity in the faction as a compromise, and as Ayn Rand wrote, "In any compromise between good and evil, it is only evil that can profit." She had also wrote, "The spread of evil is the symptom of a vacuum. Whenever evil wins, it is only by default: by the moral failure of those who evade the fact that there can be no compromise on basic principles," much akin to the Edmund *Burke quote that many like to use, in this instance of government out of control, it is the people that have evacuated political philosophy, causing vacuum. It is this vacuum that have allowed the federalists of both conservative parties to branch off as liberal and conservative, the people, instead of objectively looking at the facts, took their word for it, and in a free society there is no greater moral failing than to not think for oneself.*

# 3     Conservatism, what is it really?

Conservative is a liquid word, it spans time only by its own malleability, what is traditional in 1776 is not so today, and as such this needs to be addressed and stricken from political position. Politicians who use the word to describe themselves or opponents are akin to those who use "ducktalk" in Orwell's 1984, it means praise to an ally and condemnation to an opponent, the meaning is ambivalent at best, the usage is all that is important. The best current example is when people use this word in regard to charity, the liberal notion of giving voluntarily to charity is considered by right wing politicians as conservative, and it is praise, but to the left wing it is condemnation to prefer voluntary charity over state mandated welfare, which they also call conservative. The point of all of this is really to confuse the people into not thinking at all, and using words based on intent over meaning, basically stripping education down to indoctrination.

What I postulated in my earlier article, as Conservatism, is actually Statism, as defined in Merriam-Webster[5]:

---

5 "Statism" Merriam-Webster Online Dictionary. 2009. Merriam-Webster Online. 15 March 2009

concentration of economic controls and planning in the hands of a highly centralized government often extending to government ownership of industry.  Variations on this theme are what left and right political stances are all about, both have the feature of highly centralized government, the left would have government dictate industry, the right would have the opposite, industry dictating government.

## 4    The Looming Hand of Statism

Now with a clear idea of what Liberalism and Statism are, let us review how the political climate can come into view with a diagram; imagine if you will an equilateral triangle:

---

http://www.merriam webster.com/dictionary/statism

# Liberalism

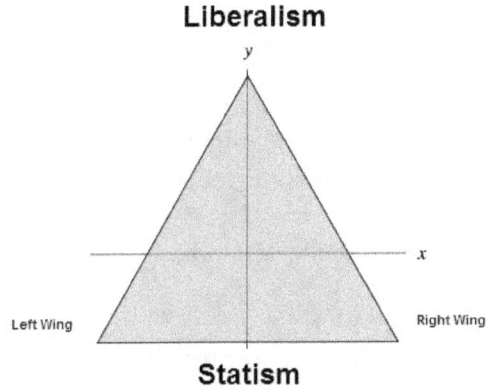

## Statism

Now, the "y" axis represents Liberalism vs. Statism, and the "x" axis represents right wing and left wing politics, as we can see, the more Liberal you get the less influence the right and left have on your government. As you approach the apex of this triangle, there is less government involvement, above said apex is a concept known as anarchism, and I know, you are all thinking of kids with safety pins, but the reality is, the objective definition of anarchism is defined in Merriam-Webster[6];

---

6  "Anarchism" <u>Merriam-Webster Online Dictionary</u>. 2009. Merriam-Webster Online. 15 March 2009

http://www.merriam-webster.com/dictionary/anarchism

1 : a political theory holding all forms of governmental authority to be unnecessary and undesirable and advocating a society based on voluntary cooperation and free association of individuals and groups

2 : the advocacy or practice of anarchistic principles

So at the peak you are left with a society without a government, all based on voluntary involvement, and as you scroll down into the triangle, you lose Liberalism to Statism, the founders did not disagree with some government, just as little as possible to remain a nation free from other nation's rule and simultaneously a people free from its nation's rule.

The problem with the left and right influences on the society is that they themselves want more influence, they want more power, and in a liberal government, there is a maximum amount of influence they can have.  The remedy to this end is to build arguments with each other that will increase Statism to solve the contention without compromising their own current level of influence.  These arguments are long in list and meaningless to individual freedom, save for the fact that they all look to distract you from the loss of liberty, spending money is a perfect example, both left and right wish to spend your money in different sinkholes, neither really discusses you keeping your wealth.  So out of self interest the left and right will quibble with each other in order to derive an emotional response from the people, this emotional state is the goal, because emotional people are irrational and will graciously hand over liberty in order to have their way temporarily, and cannot be convinced that a loss of liberty in their personal interest will someday return on them as the whim of society changes.

## 5    Where are all the Liberals?

As I previously explained, Liberalism is not currently existent in major partisan politics, so with that said where are all the people represented by views that match liberalism, do they have a party, or are they deceived into thinking that major partisan politics cover the ideals defining Liberalism?  I think these questions are best answered in viewing third parties and those who choose the lesser of two evils; these people are disenfranchised by partisan left and right issues and are trying to halt or reverse the Statism occurring due to these issues.

Third parties, not all but a few, are centered around constitutional government, the idea that government is *best* which *governs least*, as stated by Thomas Paine, in the premier of these third parties are the Constitutionalist and Libertarian.  Constitutionalists are, as far as I can tell, the religious wing of the Liberal movement[7], while the Libertarians are more concerned with secular liberty, leaving religion as a private issue[8]. Good comes from both these groups as they are dedicated to the Constitution, and a Liberal (small) government, based on the principles of the republic, the only real definitive issue is the secular issue. The Constitution Party's platform page alienates many of it's would be supporters as it states: "The Constitution Party gratefully acknowledges the blessing of our Lord and Savior Jesus Christ as Creator, Preserver and Ruler of the Universe and of these United States. We hereby appeal to Him for mercy, aid, comfort, guidance and the protection of His Providence as we work to restore and preserve these United States." I firmly believe it does not take a brain surgeon to understand how one can feel alienated, as I support Constitutional Principles, but am not a Christian, nor do I "acknowledge Jesus as Creator". I feel that the Constitution party may have the interests of the constitution in mind, but to attach their dogma to their politics is a mistake the founders themselves warned against. Libertarians, on the other hand are more open, leaving religion out of the equation of their politics, as their

---

7 Constitution Party Homepage
http://www.constitutionparty.com/

8 Libertarian Party Homepage  http://www.lp.org/

principles state, "We hold that all individuals have the right to exercise sole dominion over their own lives, and have the right to live in whatever manner they choose, so long as they do not forcibly interfere with the equal right of others to live in whatever manner they choose." Now yes, the Constitution Party states that it is ok to not worship Christ, but it leaves the thought in my mind, and probably anyone that is not a Christian, that ascension is capped for any of us based on religious persuasion. This leads me to the conclusion that the Constitution Party, though their hearts are in good intent, cling avidly to the left right issue of religion, which dooms it, once in power, to generate Statism. The Libertarian Party would be left standing as the truly Liberal party, looking for the least intrusion into the people's lives, with no left right issue to fuel any Statism what so ever.

The lesser of two evils voters I believe are more interested in halting the growth of government in a way that is not aligned with their personal left right issue, unfortunately, they are so polarized between differing ideologies as to which Statism is better, they forget that Statism is not the Constitutional way. By selfish interest that will not unite at limiting the government, as they do not mind if it grows their way, becoming emotional about what government should govern over, and as postulated before doom themselves when the social pendulum swings out of their favor. The other people in this group are the ones that finally understand that partisan politics is an issue, though I will not go out on a limb and claim they understand true Liberalism yet, they are at least showing signs that growth is still possible, and liberty is never out of reach, the outrage has to just reach a breaking point for each individual. These republicans and democrats that have walked freely away from their party, in realization that they are not represented, need to find out why, classify the issues, and come to the attention that it is a left and right issue meant to increase the power of the federal government. They must decide is it better to be free, or run the hazard of the opposing wing of politics to have the power they grant to their wing?

## 6     The Four Philosophies Political Theory

In regards to politics, I have shown the political spectrum as a triangle (shown below) and reasoned the philosophies attached as Liberalism, Statism, Left Wing and Right Wing.

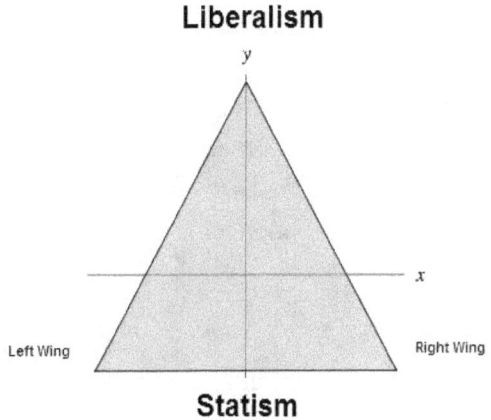

**Liberalism**

**Statism**

Three of the four, all but liberalism, share the feature of increased government, in most versions, to the annihilation of the individual, liberalism stands alone as the only philosophy that promotes individualism, I intend to answer the questions; what is the objective definitions and goals of each of these political philosophies, what are the features of each of these philosophies in comparison to their diametric opposites and which is best for most people, through objective reasoning.

## 7      Jokers to the Left, Clowns to the Right

The left and right wings of politics are available to be observed in every nation, though in America, unlike foreign nations, we refuse to call these concepts what they truly are, it is seemingly taboo in major media, and as such have worked their way out of common sense in the American people. It is necessary to identify these concepts as they are in earnest if we are to discuss them rationally, and since this has not been prevalent in modern America, I can only assume that the best one can hope for is an irrational voting pool, though more common would seem to be absent voters.

So what is the Left exactly? In every instance outside of America the left is designated as the Communist or Labor Party. In the United States it is called the Democrat Party, one would assume that if this is the case, the left here should line up with communism. Let us look at the objective definition of Communism and the platform of the Democrat Party:

Merriam-Webster: Communism[9]

Main Entry: com·mu·nism

Pronunciation: \ˈkäm-yə-ˌni-zəm, -yü-\

---

9 "Communism" (2009). In *Merriam-Webster Online Dictionary*. Retrieved March 24, 2009, from

http://www.merriam-webster.com/dictionary/communism

Function: *noun*

Etymology: French *communisme,* from *commun* common

Date: 1840

1 a: a theory advocating elimination of private property b: a system in which goods are owned in common and are available to all as needed

2 *capitalized* a: a doctrine based on revolutionary Marxian socialism and Marxism-Leninism that was the official ideology of the Union of Soviet Socialist Republics b: a totalitarian system of government in which a single authoritarian party controls state-owned means of production c: a final stage of society in Marxist theory in which the state has withered away and economic goods are distributed equitably d: communist systems collectively

The Democrat Party Platform in short from their site[10]

The Democratic Party has a long and proud history of representing and protecting the interests of working Americans and guaranteeing personal liberties for all. One

---

10 The Democratic Party Website, "Our Party" tab, "What we Stand for" bar
http://www.democrats.org/a/party/stand.html

of the places we articulate our beliefs is in the Party's National Platform, adopted every four years by the Delegates at the National Convention.

(Long form located here
http://www.democrats.org/a/party/platform.html )

Now I know the Platform seems quite innocuous in the short order, but when we delve into the I-paper, expanded, version of the platform, it becomes a little more eerie, a lot more similar to the 1 b definition of Communism, which is the ends to Marxism's means so to speak. "Today, we pledge a return to core moral principles like stewardship, service to others, personal responsibility, shared sacrifice and a fair shot for all ..." (Pg. 6) "We need a government that stands up for the hopes, values, and interests of working people..." (Pg. 8) "health care should be a shared responsibility between employers, workers, insurers, providers and government..." (Pg. 10) "...behavioral health management should be assured for all Americans who require care coordination... ...We should promote additional tobacco and substance abuse prevention." (Pg. 11) "...making sure workers get their fair share..." (Pg. 14), these quotes from the above link provided with the

Democratic Party platform, are quite reminiscent of the definition of Marxism[11]

Main Entry: Marx·ism

Pronunciation: \'märk-ˌsi-zəm\

Function: *noun*

Date: 1887

: the political, economic, and social principles and policies advocated by Marx ; *especially* : a theory and practice of socialism including the labor theory of value, dialectical materialism, the class struggle, and dictatorship of the proletariat until the establishment of a classless society

Further I would like to point out Karl Marx's 10 planks[12]:

---

11 "Marxism" (2009). In *Merriam-Webster Online Dictionary*. Retrieved March 24, 2009, from http://www.merriam-webster.com/dictionary/Marxism

12 Communist Manifesto, Marx 1848, referenced the 10 points from Wikipedia Article on the subject for ease of examination, http://en.wikipedia.org/wiki/Communist_Manifesto#10_Conditions_For_Transition_To_Communism

1. Abolition of private property and the application of all rents of land to public purposes.
2. A heavy progressive or graduated income tax.
3. Abolition of all rights of inheritance.
4. Confiscation of the property of all emigrants and rebels.
5. Centralization of credit in the hands of the state, by means of a national bank with State capital and an exclusive monopoly.
6. Centralization of the means of communications and transportation in the hands of the State.
7. Extension of factories and instruments of production owned by the state, the bringing into cultivation of wastelands, and the improvement of the soil generally in accordance with a common plan.
8. Equal liability of all to labor. Establishment of industrial armies, especially for agriculture.
9. Combination of agriculture with manufacturing industries, gradual abolition of the distinction between town and country, by a more equitable distribution of population over the country.
10. Free education for all children in public schools. Abolition of children's factory labor in its present form. Combination of education with industrial production.

You will note the appearance of "labor theory value" and "dictatorship of the proletariat" in the definition of

Marxism, and the few selections are indicative of the entire platform of the Democratic Party. One would think that Democratic and Labor would be completely interchangeable under objective inspection of the definitions surrounding communism and the Democratic platform. Democratic Party policy follows left wing authoritarianism based on the moral high ground of "serving the masses" just as Marxism justifies the "dictatorship of the proletariat" in the effort to establish a "classless society". I would also like to note for all those who believe that the Marx ideal would abolish a government, this is just not true, it would abolish classes, no one would be rich or poor as all would have equal share to all resources, the issue with this is that as population increases resources diminish and the ruling class would always exist, able to extort resources with the power of political pull. The parallels between the concept of Marxist Communism and the Democratic Party platform are well established and apparent, it is to the point that they do not even hide it, knowing that the indoctrination of the people would not allow them to see such a parallel. Which brings us to our other more sinister parallel the moral justification for the annihilation of the individual in the name of the "greater good"? As seen from the quotes above, the focus is on the sacrifice of the individual for the rest of the society, making it the moral imperative of the individual to sacrifice himself to the community, and personal achievement is discounted unless it has social benefit and is given freely to society.

Another inherently communist government body is the UN; I will now direct you to the universal declaration of human rights for my proof, as it is similar along the lines of Communism and Democratic Platform[13]

## "Article 22.

Everyone, as a member of society, has the right to social security and is entitled to realization, through national effort and international co-operation and in accordance with the organization and resources of each State, of the economic, social and cultural rights indispensable for his dignity and the free development of his personality."

## "Article 23.

**(3) Everyone who works has the right to just and favourable remuneration ensuring for himself and his family an existence worthy of human dignity, and supplemented, if necessary, by other means of social protection."**

## "Article 24.

---

13 UN Declaration of Human Rights, adopted 1948
http://www.un.org/Overview/rights.html

Everyone has the right to rest and leisure, including reasonable limitation of working hours and periodic holidays with pay."

## "Article 25.

(1) Everyone has the right to a standard of living adequate for the health and well-being of himself and of his family, including food, clothing, housing and medical care and necessary social services..."

## "Article 26.

(1) Everyone has the right to education. Education shall be free, at least in the elementary and fundamental stages. Elementary education shall be compulsory.

(2) Education... shall further the activities of the United Nations for the maintenance of peace."

## "Article 29.

Everyone has duties to the community in which alone the free and full development of his personality is possible.

So as we can see the apparent left wing bend in the moral superiority of the greater good is a fundamental role of the United Nations, and it leaves little to the imagination that the authority is not upon the individual to live his life but rather to the community. Expanded to the international community with the UN, one can only imagine the standard of living when free competition for goods and services is replaced by this system worldwide, which coincidentally or maybe not so much, was what Marx prophesized with his philosophy of communism, a worldwide expansion.  It seems that the UN is making Marx's dream a reality, through international authority, which according to its charter it was always intended to have [14]in a military sense.

In America the Right Wing movement is represented by the Republican Party in its major political theater, in opposition to the Left Wing Democrats, which represents a set of values that is commonly referred to as "Conservative".  The movement uses subtle euphemisms to get their platform across to the voters, one must ask, what are the ends to these means and, more importantly, why are they using this political tactic?  As noted below, the Republican Platform stands on a nationalist foundation, the idea that we as people should line up behind the government, lead by them, and unite for the national cause.  This ideology is focused on producing a nationalist movement, cleverly disguised as patriotism, to move towards the logical conclusion, a fascist government.  The subtlety, which is proper to America, is very relevant to this end, and it is required that we examine why.  Fascism is an unpopular concept in the United States; there are two main reasons why this could be, both quite sufficient to warrant the subtlety; the human atrocities attributed to fascism, and its

---

14 UN Charter Chapter VII
http://www.un.org/aboutun/charter/chapter7.shtml

role in the propagation of the Second World War. The death toll was a record high in the hands of fascism, until after World War II, when the communist nations began weighing in. In truth, Stalin's Soviet Administration exterminated more than 3 times the amount of people fascism had in total. The only reasonable answer as why fascism overshadows communism in political negativity, and so the need for subtlety, is in reality the propensity for war. A fascist regime must rely on war, a constant enemy, in order to maintain the nationalism in the population allowing for its particular excesses. Remember not that they are subtle, but rather why, and this is because the ends to their means is a totalitarian fascist regime, demanding obedience through nationalist fervor.

What is the Right? In many nations the right movement is embodied in the Nationalist (Fascist) Party, in America we call the Right wing party the Republican Party, just as with the Democrats and the Left, one could assume there is a correlation in the two. Let us compare Nationalism and Fascism, and see how they weigh against the Republican Party platform.

Merriam-Webster: Nationalism[15]

Main Entry: na·tion·al·ism

Pronunciation: \ˈnash-nə-ˌli-zəm, ˈna-shə-nə-ˌli-zəm\

Function: *noun*

Date: 1844

1: loyalty and devotion to a nation; *especially*: a sense of national consciousness exalting one nation above all others and placing primary emphasis on promotion of its culture and interests as opposed to those of other nations or supranational groups

2: a nationalist movement or government

Merriam-Webster: Fascism[16]

Main Entry: fas·cism

---

15 "Nationalism" (2009). In *Merriam-Webster Online Dictionary*. Retrieved April 3, 2009, from http://www.merriam-webster.com/dictionary/nationalism

16 "Fascism" (2009). In *Merriam-Webster Online Dictionary*. Retrieved April 3, 2009, from http://www.merriam-webster.com/dictionary/fascism

Pronunciation: \\'fa-ˌshi-zəm *also* 'fa-ˌsi-\\

Function: *noun*

Etymology: Italian *fascismo,* from *fascio* bundle, fasces, group, from Latin *fascis* bundle & *fasces*

Date: 1921

1 *often capitalized*: a political philosophy, movement, or regime (as that of the Fascisti) that exalts nation and often race above the individual and that stands for a centralized autocratic government headed by a dictatorial leader, severe economic and social regimentation, and forcible suppression of opposition

2: a tendency toward or actual exercise of strong autocratic or dictatorial control <early instances of army *fascism* and brutality — J. W. Aldridge>

The Republican Party Platform[17]

Nationalism and Fascism are truly the same concept; Fascism is in reality a refining of the nationalist movement, adding an autocratic government with strict government

---

17 Republican Party Platform
http://www.gop.com/2008Platform/

regulation of all aspects of the individual's life. Many of the "successful" Fascist movements (I say this to mean they came to full power) have emphasized national identity (Italy) or racial identity and purity (Germany), and exhibited all the trappings of a Fascist society, down to the oppression of dissent. Now how does this relate to the Republican Party? Well, if you refer to the primary site listed in Footnote (18) you will see the first note in the platform is National Security, national security is a very nationalist concept, it is the safety of the nation above all others. Going to the link for National Security[18] we find a plethora of Nationalist ideals fit for an American Fascist regime:

"(Peace through strength) requires the unity of Americans"

"All Americans should affirm that our first obligation is the security of our country."

"The fact that eighty percent of our critical infrastructure is in private hands highlights the need for public-private partnerships to safeguard it"

---

18

http://www.gop.com/2008Platform/NationalSecurity.htm#

"In our multiethnic nation, everyone – immigrants and native-born alike – must embrace our core values"

"In any war of ideas, our values will triumph."

It is not too much of a stretch to see the Republican standard is a Nationalist policy, focusing on the superiority of our nation and the need of the whole of the populace to fall in line. Appearing in the same section: "In dealing with present conflicts and future crises, our next president must preserve all options. It would be presumptuous to specify them in advance and foolhardy to rule out any action deemed necessary for our security." We see that the Republican Party is specifically, with the expansive power of the US military machine, standing on the platform of giving the full powers of war to the executive branch. The most underlying similarity between Republican "Values" and Fascism is the annihilation of the individual under the banner of Nationalism, that the nation takes precedence over the individual.

I think there is sufficient proof to claim a definitive alignment with left and right wing politics, between America and the rest of the world, the only logical conclusion is that the radicals of each here at home are looking for their personal ideals (Communism and Fascism, respectively) to be implemented. The less radical politicians are more often falling between the far left and far right with no lateral movement towards Liberalism.

# 8    Public Good vs. National Security

Now that we truly have a basis of understanding of the left and the right, let us compare and contrast the two, these policies should have differing results, as they are diametric opposites of the political scale. The left, or Communist, faction is driven for the sole purpose of the "greater" or "public" good, and the collective is morally superior to the individual by virtue of the fact that it is best for all. This is the collectivist notion that the group is more important than the individual, that rights are assigned by "class" or other segregatory demographic such as race, heritage, gender, lifestyle, etc. Most of the current incarnation of these ideas is rooted in post-Marx writings about communism sources from the Frankfurt Institute for Social Research[19], when the worldwide proletariat revolution did not take place. This is the basis for the current communist movement in the United States: collective civil rights, politically correct speech and egalitarian social policies, all

---

19 Frankfurt Institute website - History Page
http://www.ifs.uni-frankfurt.de/english/history.htm

indicated as the foundation of the Democratic Party platform.

The Right, or Fascist, faction is represented by the Nationalist notion of National Security, that our nation is under constant threat from foreign and domestic enemies, and if you "love your country" you will fall in line and do as you are told. We had seen the greatest display of this during the last few years when the P.A.T.R.I.O.T. U.S.A. Act was being enforced, where members of our own society decided that if you were a patriot you should be silent about government intrusions. Where not patriotic, but rather nationalist, fervor swept across the land giving silent consent to the loss of liberty, the individual did not feel concerned about it as Nationalist pride encourages the individual to trust the government. The current platform is no different, espousing dissent as unpatriotic, not falling in line with their values is agreeing with the "enemy" and all who disagree are destroying America.

In unison, both parties will distinctly say that the ideology of their party platform cannot be realized in America, the "It cannot happen here" mentality, the blatant lie that the parties claim to be for liberty and communism/fascism is what everyone else is doing. This ties into the quote by Goethe, "None are more *hopelessly enslaved* than those who falsely believe they are free."[20]  Both political ideologies are against the individual, as are the party ideals: there can be no individual in collectivism or nationalism, so each has the feature of the annihilation of the individual. They both expect to destroy the free thought process in favor of a group mentality, either under the theory of the "greater good" or "national security" which in turn will melt away the individual.  The Group will be all-important, rights or better put in these ideals, privileges are granted in relation to the size of one's group or the majority will.

The end result in either case is tyranny, where the elite direct the lives of the people in an Orwellian fashion; in the perfect case it has an elegant mixture of collectivism and nationalism to deceive the people into a stupor.  In the end the wings are a means to a common goal, a Statist Oligarchy, where the individual is annihilated and the people as a group live and die at the will of the government.

---

20
http://www.brainyquote.com/quotes/quotes/j/johannwolf134023.html

# 9    The Individual versus the State

The real opposition with government is not a left/right issue it is an "up/down" one, about more or less individual liberty, it is the difference between Liberalism and Statism, the power of the individual against the power of the state. As demonstrated previously, the left/right issues only serve the purpose of taking liberty from individuals in exchange for empowering the state, the end result being the annihilation of the individual.  Where do you place value is the question, do you value the liberty to live your life without depriving the life or liberty from others or would you rather have the state oppress your life through legislation?

Liberalism is the label of individual liberty expressed in government, a society of individuals who can agree that liberty is the rule of the land, and the government is assigned few and nominal tasks.  This is not a lawless society, but a society with laws that the entire population can draw back to the basic human rights.  This is to say; not violating another's rights is not violating the law and violating the law means separation from society.  The republic[21] is the embodiment of this society, as described in

---

21 "Republic" (2009). In *Merriam-Webster Online Dictionary*. Retrieved April 12, 2009, from http://www.merriam-webster.com/dictionary/republic

the United States Constitution, very reminiscent of the primary republic of ancient Rome, after the monarchy was overthrown, known as Res Publica Romana.

Merriam-Webster: Republic

Main Entry: re·pub·lic

Function: *noun*

Etymology: French *république,* from Middle French *republique,* from Latin *respublica,* from *res* thing, wealth + *publica,* feminine of *publicus* public

Date: 1604

1 a (1): a government having a chief of state who is not a monarch and who in modern times is usually a president (2): a political unit (as a nation) having such a form of government b (1): a government in which supreme power resides in a body of citizens entitled to vote and is exercised by elected officers and representatives responsible to them and governing according to law (2): a political unit (as a nation) having such a form of government c: a usually specified republican government of a political unit <the French Fourth *Republic*>

2: a body of persons freely engaged in a specified activity <the *republic* of letters>

3: a constituent political and territorial unit of the former nations of Czechoslovakia, the Union of Soviet Socialist Republics, or Yugoslavia

As we can see the definition b (1) is the only objective entry, a government that rules according to the law and the power resides in the hands of the citizens who have the right to vote.  The laws of this ancient republic were written in stone, the civil rights could not be tampered with and were respected by the governing Senate and Plebeian Council, this is the "republican form of government" guaranteed by the Constitution[22].  The Bill of Rights[23] is the enumeration of the rights the government should never trespass against; these first ten Amendments to the Constitution truly list the boundaries of a government for the United States and advocate the power of the individual

---

22 US Constitution Article IV Section 4  "The United States shall guarantee to every State in this Union a Republican Form of Government"
http://www.archives.gov/exhibits/charters/constitution_transcript.html

23 US Constitution Bill Of Rights
http://www.archives.gov/exhibits/charters/bill_of_rights_transcript.html

to hold this government accountable if it were ever to overstep its boundaries. This is why the founders are referred to as liberals, because they created a government that was held to respect the rights of the individual and individual liberty, therefore they created a Republic.

As we look to the opposite of Liberalism we will find the gradual decline into a tyrannical government system known as Statism, the left and right versions of this are negligible because the individual looses liberty either way. Statism is represented in total by the Oligarchy[24], defined below as a government by the few, despite the concurrence with the corruption that is mentioned, oligarchic government is a small group that exercises control over the population.

Merriam-Webster: oligarchy

Main Entry: ol·i·gar·chy

 Function: *noun*

Date: 1542

---

24 "Oligarchy" (2009). In *Merriam-Webster Online Dictionary*. Retrieved April 12, 2009, from http://www.merriam-webster.com/dictionary/oligarchy

1: government by the few

2: a government in which a small group exercises control especially for corrupt and selfish purposes; *also*: a group exercising such control

3: an organization under oligarchic control

The laws of an oligarchy do not hold the governing powers accountable; this is a very Machiavellian form of government, where the ends justify the means, where the rule of law is the rule of the time. Representative Democracies are often oligarchies, where the representatives are elected, empowered by the majority and require a majority of representatives to change the law of the land. Remember that no law, not even a basic human right, is safe in this form of government, if the right to speak against the government is not popular then speaking against the government is illegal. In order for the oligarchy to enforce its power on the people, it must control all aspects of the average person's life, where what you see, what you read, verily what you know is subject to litigation. This form of government is reminiscent of the monarchies of old, where the few decided the very fate of the individual, where the whim of nobility was applicable as the law.

# 10    Democracy, the God of the Oligarchy

Currently, an oligarchy is a government of complacent consent; the "herd" mentality is praised over the individual to propagate a tyranny of the majority, where the 51st percentile decides the level of freedom for all.  It is the idea that the best for most is the best for all; this is the representation of the annihilation of the individual, truly considered a high crime in a republic where individual liberty trumps the state.

Merriam-Webster: Democracy (5)[25]

Main Entry: de·moc·ra·cy

Function: *noun*

Etymology: Middle French *democratie,* from Late Latin *democratia,* from Greek *dēmokratia,* from *dēmos* + *-kratia - cracy*

Date: 1576

---

25 "Democracy" (2009). In *Merriam-Webster Online Dictionary.* Retrieved April 12, 2009, from http://www.merriam-webster.com/dictionary/democracy

1 a: government by the people; *especially*: rule of the majority b: a government in which the supreme power is vested in the people and exercised by them directly or indirectly through a system of representation usually involving periodically held free elections

2: a political unit that has a democratic government

3 *capitalized*: the principles and policies of the Democratic Party in the United States <from emancipation Republicanism to New Deal *Democracy* — C. M. Roberts>

4: the common people especially when constituting the source of political authority

5: the absence of hereditary or arbitrary class distinctions or privileges


Objectively the democracy is the rule of the majority, so by design people would have to organize in voting blocks to gain a majority in society in order to have true representation of their beliefs. What normally happens in this case is a compromise of morality, a choosing of the "lesser of two evils", one who agrees with the most important issues, but usually not with many others. On the national level these voting blocs will take a singular issue and bind together in a Nationalist or Collectivist voting bloc, completely compromising their ideals for one issue that they value, usually in a herd this size we are talking about the emotional response to the opposition party. The best current example is the enormous amount of people who voted Democrat because they were not Republican, and really not considering anything else.

The representative democracy is what the oligarchy truly stems from, where democratically elected representatives are granted the supreme power of the people by volition of election. The idea is that the people can vote the person out in the next election, but while they are in office their power is of the people, surrendered at the voting booth. Representative Democracies often polarize the voting blocs to generate infighting, allowing the government to act unnoticed, by choosing a left or right issue to be the cornerstone of the party platform. The people who voted for the "winner" feel empowered and often disregard the rights of the people who did not vote for their candidate, attributing complaints as "sore loser syndrome". The reality is the representatives are not bound by their campaign promises (examples: Bush Sr., Clinton, Bush Jr., Obama) and only have to placate the majority of their constituency to secure re-election. The majority can be fooled by candidates who support campaign promises in word and by supporting legislative measures, but working with other representatives to have the majority vote against these pieces of legislation.

With a democracy, you are always doomed to the path of oligarchy; even with the best intentions in mind, giving any power to the government is taking away from your individual liberty and therefore your personal role in the society as a whole. One should always question the placement of public trust, it is a powerful tool and the abuse of it has a catastrophic result on the population, genocide, one that in almost all cases comes to fruition.

# 11    Politics Illustrated

Now, with all the information provided we can correct the previous political diagram to demonstrate the reality a little better than what we are used to seeing.

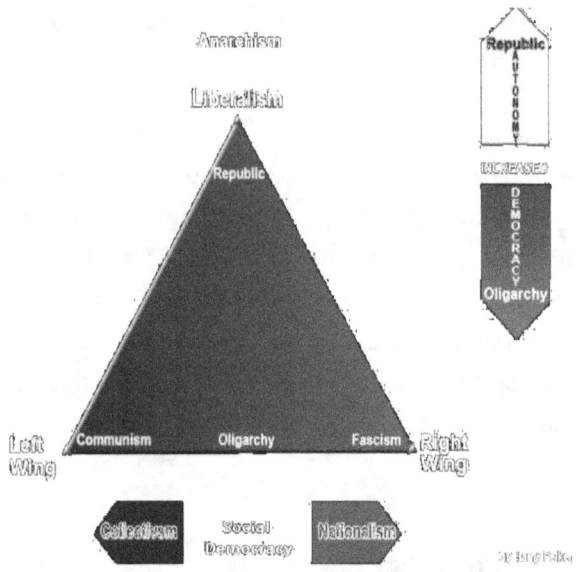

This diagram[26] is supported by all my logical claims, the references and real world examples, as the correct view of politics, the left (Collectivist) and right (Nationalist) issues, the Liberalism (Autonomy) and Statism (Democracy) battle for power and the forms of government that these political stances generate (Republic, Oligarchy - Social Democracies, Fascist and Communist Regimes).

---

26 Graphic Created with help from Carl Cline

## What Does Freedom Demand?

## Freedom Is Not Free

Every individual who has sought freedom from an oppressor knows precisely that "Freedom is not Free" is representative of their endless perseverance against their own tyrants. What does this quote really mean to the reasonable person, politicians have used this to justify foreign intervention, but this is senseless, how does the freedom a country enjoys be dependent of fighting oppressors in foreign lands? This concept implies that there are inconveniences one must endure to prevent and stop tyranny at home, freedom demands, in maintenance, a price in time and energy, which takes two forms, passive resistance and aggressive resistance. Passive resistance includes, but is not limited to, informing and educating people why resistance is necessary, civil disobedience, organizing and participating in peaceable protest. I would like to believe aggressive resistance is self explanatory, but for the sake of clarity, this tactic includes insurgency and violent revolution. Both of these tactics require a tremendous investment of time and energy; organizing, spreading the word, equipping, etc, this is the price of freedom. Verily, the monetary cost of resistance is also an indicator of the price of freedom.

"Do you want to know who you are? Don't ask. Act! Action will delineate and define you."
Thomas Jefferson[27]

Simply knowing that there is something wrong is not enough, instinct overrides reason if one does not expend the energy to explore and identify this malady, and use

---

27
http://www.brainyquote.com/quotes/quotes/t/thomasjeff120901.html

knowledge to judge the best course of action. Think of wild animals, when nature is about to unleash itself upon an area instinctively the animals move away and flee the area, as humans however, fleeing is not the only option against forces that threaten us, we can act upon reason. Reason leave us as humans two options for action, fight or flight, we can choose to stand up against the issue and figure a way to overcome it, or we can choose to flee for a society that has no such issue. Knowing that there is something wrong is not enough; if you have the knowledge that there is a problem and do not act you are accepting the flawed society and the oppression that invariably comes with it. It is only what you do with that knowledge, which is where the power is, in the implementation of the knowledge, not in merely having it. When you know something is wrong (no Power), you can act, you can identify it (Power of Perception), you can announce it (Power of Declaration) and you can neutralize it (Power of Destruction) or you can choose to not act at all and remain powerless. You use your knowledge to direct your action, your knowledge is your weapon, lying dormant and acting upon that knowledge is effectively lifting the weapon and using it, giving it the power. I am sure some have come to the conclusion that, at this point I am only speaking of violence, I wish to remind people of the adage the "pen is mightier that the sword" ones word is a weapon as well as ones fist. One can destroy tyranny with either words or arms; the only commonality of these two tactics is the use of the primary weapon, the human mind, knowledge, and without such you leave one tyrant only to deliver yourself into a new oppression.

## Freedom is Responsibility

The responsible person takes their freedom very seriously, they guard it from all oppressors, and they extend their vigilance to the rest of their society as a loss of liberty to any member of a society can, and often does revert back unto them.  The irresponsible person takes their freedom for granted, expects others to be inconvenienced and often finds themselves without liberty in a reasonably short time, as with most cases, without their life as well, as they well should.  It is very easy, there is no "cost" to being irresponsible, it requires no prior investment, however there is a price, the loss of what one is irresponsible with. This is very true in the case of liberty; the responsible person heeds the words of wise men before him:

"Guard with jealous attention the public liberty. Suspect everyone who approaches that jewel."

Patrick Henry[28]

The men responsible for the American Revolution also mentioned those that are irresponsible with their liberty in quotes such as this:

"That which we obtain too easily, we esteem too lightly."

Thomas Paine[29]

When a people are drawn to irresponsibility, not only out of ease, but usually coaxed to it by their own government, they begin to take for granted the freedom that they once had high respect for. They become complacent and then apathetic, the final stage of irresponsibility before all responsibility for your life is placed in the hands of an

---

28

http://www.brainyquote.com/quotes/quotes/p/patrickhen101581.html

29

http://www.brainyquote.com/quotes/quotes/t/thomaspain159458.html

oppressor, and with that great irresponsibility comes the loss of all power.  The complacent are ruled, they do not decide their life, it is chosen for them and if they decide to turn from this they are punished gravely.


With everything I write I cannot force you to follow, agree or read, I can only ask and give the choice to you, the audience, and this is the greatest reward of freedom, the freedom to choose your own path.  You can choose to be a responsible person with your freedom, give the time and energy preserving which freedom demands, or you can choose to not, be irresponsible with your freedom, and risk losing it.  Freedom is a concept that has the seed of its own destruction planted well within it, the choice, you can choose wisely, and despite the demands, live free, or you may choose poorly and risk oppression.

So, my reader, my audience, my fan or my foe, the ball is in your court, make your choice.

# Taxed Enough, I am not too sure

On this 4<sup>th</sup> of July, there has been much saber rattling about more T.E.A. Parties across these United States, and although I do appreciate the people involved taking the time out to speak up against the government, I have a nagging thought.  Now all this protesting is good, it lets the people know that taxation is not consented, but it only goes so far, exactly what else are you doing?  What are you changing about your own life in order to get from under the Statist boot of taxation?

I am sitting here, puffing my pipe, awaiting tobacco seeds, this is my form of protest, among others I have planned in order to show the government that I do not appreciate the tax and overspend policies.  To show the monopoly government I do not want them involved in my life, there is only one way to do so without violence, to cut their funding, whether you advocate true Libertarianism (Anarchism) or limited government (Minarchism) you cannot escape this logic.  The government does not have to listen to your groups of people on the side of the street, waving their signs that were assembled from taxed goods; they are still getting their taxes.  If you are claiming that you are "Taxed Enough Already" why are you not seeking methods to get out from under taxation?

The MSM machine already played its hand, it marginalized the tax protests, with absolute success, and the monopoly in the United States followed suit, it became much ado about nothing, and opened ridicule in the name of "tea bagging". Is this the success you were hoping for, to have Rachel Maddow have a segment that basically equates anyone involved in the protests with an act that involves testicles being dipped into things? If this was the case, you all might as well have signs that state, "I'm going to dip my balls in it!" This is not what you wanted, I am certain, and with this failure to really get anything that you did want, that is, lowering of taxation and spending or cessation of more taxation in the least, the fallacy of this tactic is blearing.

So what can you do, when shouting from your soapbox will not have an effect, what do you do when you shout in the face of a deaf adversary? Gandhi had done something, in the midst of all the protesting, he had urged his people to not buy the goods from Britain, therefore undermining the monetary grasp that English men had on India. Why are you not doing anything of the like, many of us do not want to come to blows with our fellow Americans, so why not retract the means for the government to spend?

We could be seeking ways to sidestep taxation, of course I am suggesting within the legal confines, in order to send a real message to the monopoly government, let them know by decreased revenue. Stop spending, this is the simplest explanation, your dog is biting the hand that feeds him, do not feed him any longer. I am not suggesting that you go on a hunger strike or curb your habits to not give the government money, but rather, use an untaxed means to live your life unchanged. You can grow your own food, now I do understand that not all food consumption can be easily grown, but why not do what you can, every little bit is less the government can rake you for. Drying and preserving home grown food makes them available when they cannot be grown, this solves the issue of seasonal growth. I am preparing to grow my own tobacco, if you are a smoker, this is absolutely a valid form of protest, and in light of the current imperial sway it is $1000/yr (only calculating the increase) they are losing from me alone. Cut your energy and gas consumption, most of the price on energy and gas goes directly to the federal government, despite the people who blame the oil companies, it is tax that increases the price of energy. I would suggest solar power, but I know this is an expensive option, so I do leave it off the list for now.

I understand that all this may be an inconvenience, but it is convenience that enslaves you, so in contradiction, the inconvenience may be the road to freedom, are you worth your salt?  Are you willing to do what is necessary to let the government know, you have had enough?  Are you going to, instead of becoming more parody fuel for propagandist media, send a striking message to the government, in the only way they will feel it?  If you wish to let the government know you have been taxed enough already, STOP SPENDING, STOP FEEDING THE LIBERTY EATING MONSTER, turn your back on him, and let him starve.

I would like to add I am very disappointed that I felt there was a need for this article, the standard by this point among the tax protesters is mysteriously not to cut federal funding, they will go to Walmart to buy supplies and drive to a street to scream at traffic, but they will not bother to make the necessary adjustments in their lives to send a message that cannot be ignored.  I envision an America that is not so weak as to allow themselves to be subjugated by their possessions, by convenience, we have passed the time to step up to the plate.  Will you be a bench warmer, or will you hit your message out of the park?

# Chapter 3: Anarchism

In the midst of working on Liberal vs. Conservative, due to the suggestion, albeit persistent, as I am quite hard headed at times, of my wife, I had begun actively participating in the Mises Institute Community[30] in order to expand my knowledge in free market economics and capitalism. I had broad ideas but had neglected the research in this area; I had made the conscious decision to continue my education there, looking to the contributors for guidance. Much of the contentions of the other social networks were not present there, I had gone there with my preconceived notions and they applied reasonable debate to them. I had read a lot in the first few weeks of interaction, both on the message boards and the suggested reading offered to me by the other members of the community. The Mises Community was and still is a wealth of knowledge, not only in the field of economics, but history and philosophy as well, a good deal of the participants not only willing but eager as vocational seekers of truths to help educate any who are willing to ask questions. The community was not perfect, though there was a consistent production of logical debate, as with all forum communities, some people were attracted with the purpose of ad hominem attacking ideas outside their comfort zone.

---

30 http://mises.org/Community/

My many friends at the Mises Community had directed me to a good deal of work by current and past Austrian School economists, and most importantly, my wife directed me to Lysander Spooner's "*No Treason*", I was dumbfounded, it was what a drunk refers to as a moment of clarity. Spooner's essay had destroyed the argument of consented government, legitimate taxation and voting as anything more than an act of self-defense. All remaining arguments I had reserved to retain a limited government were summarily destroyed by the logical arguments of Murray Rothbard, F.A. Hayek, Walter Block and other prominent fellows of the Mises Institute.

I had written this in the midst of Liberal vs. Conservative, I hope it clears up why, if you check my footnotes, the definition in print mismatches the definition found when following the footnote.

## Orwellian Redefinition

Those of us who are familiar with 1984 understand the concept of Newspeak....

Excerpt from Liberal vs. Conservative:

Liberalism is defined as follows by Merriam-Webster

1: the quality or state of being liberal
2 a (often capitalized): a movement in modern
Protestantism emphasizing intellectual liberty and the
spiritual and ethical content of Christianity b: a theory in
economics emphasizing individual freedom from restraint
and usually based on free competition, the self-regulating
market, and the gold standard c: a political philosophy
based on belief in progress, the essential goodness of the
human race, and the autonomy of the individual and
standing for the protection of political and civil liberties d
(capitalized) : the principles and policies of a Liberal party

This was the definition taken from Merriam-Webster in
February, and the definition was persistent, if I recall
correctly through April, though I have not referenced the
definition since then. Well in Orwellian Fashion....

This is the New Definition of Liberalism, taken from the
same dictionary, that my footnotes link to...

1: the quality or state of being liberal
2 a (often capitalized): a movement in modern
Protestantism emphasizing intellectual liberty and the
spiritual and ethical content of Christianity b: a theory in
economics emphasizing individual freedom from restraint
and usually based on free competition, the self-regulating
market, and the gold standard c: a political philosophy
based on belief in progress, the essential goodness of the

human race, and the autonomy of the individual and standing for the protection of political and civil liberties; specifically: such a philosophy that considers government as a crucial instrument for amelioration of social inequities (as those involving race, gender, or class) d capitalized: the principles and policies of a Liberal party

I think the paradox is more than obvious in the second definition, autonomy of the individual being a principle of self governance and considering the governments as a crucial instrument are not compatible in the least. I had written to Merriam-Webster about this change in the definition receiving no answer to my questions regarding a reason for the change in definition.

## The Morality Of Methodological Individualism

In its purest form the Individual is the prime exemplar of a social moralist, after stripping away all compulsory action handed down by society, it is from what the individual does by pure volition that we can measure his morality. Voluntary action by one or a group of individuals can be the only measure of the morality of a society, as each member of a society is individually responsible for his or her actions. Compulsory indebtedness through service or taxation cannot be a measure of morality, as not doing your "fair share" derives punishment for non-conformity, and being like everyone else, doing like everyone else, following the herd, is no guarantee of moral correctness. The collected group does not concern itself with morality, it presumes that morality is the majority consensus, and therefore dilutes the concepts of justice and equal rights. We can take many examples from history's most horrific events, and in each one we will find that there is a Collective that justifies these atrocities as moral. There is no moral basis in compulsory or collective action, as these remove the responsibility from the individual in both volition (compulsory) and identity (collective). It is only in voluntary individual action that we can measure morality, because it requires the individual to make a choice between a moral and an amoral action, and take full responsibility for such an action.

Take for example a man walking down a street, he encounters another man, who states he is in need of money, and would like five dollars, of course there are extenuating circumstances, but for simplicity, choosing to give or not to give is a measure of the man's morality. Now put a weapon in the second man's hand, and the first man gives money by compulsory action, conveying no sense of morality on the action, because regardless if he is willing, he must, or potentially perish. To exemplify the lack of moral measure of the collective, when a group is encountered by the same needy man, and they elect the wealthiest to give, it is not the morality of the others that the wealthiest supports, only his own, and that is only if they do not force him to give. The group could say "we" gave five dollars to a needy man on the street, but when forced to identify their individual part, only the one that parted with money voluntarily is really compassionate. Even if they all give to the needy man, it is not that they gave five dollars, but rather because they all did their part of giving voluntarily and individually that confers the morality to the group.

## The Smallest and Most Powerful Word

I, the simplest word in the English language, and simultaneously the most potent, I, the mark of the individual, takes full responsibility. I is more than just a significance of self in a sentence, but it speaks to the writer, or speaker that they are in fact conscious of themselves within the world about them. I am, I do, no other word holds the power of such a force of will. I am, nothing else in the English language truly confers ones knowledge of oneself within the world. I do, I do not, signifies control over yourself and the control one exerts on the environment about them. As the signatory of the individual, all choice is seated in the message of I, even when acting in the common goal; it is the part of each individual that represents the outcome. If we take the example of the fight for constitutional government, we do not pick up a collective pen and write these articles I post, **I** pick up **my** pen and write, as the rest have their part to play in this effort. I incurs the responsibility onto the self, to keep the example, I would be the one rewarded or punished for what I write, this is why I, the individual, not we, the collective, is the true measure of morality in a society.

## The Impeccability of Voluntary Individualism

The individual acting voluntarily is in fact impeccable, that is flawless, one takes full responsibility of one's actions and makes all moral decisions based on what is right for them, if this is not the case then there is no moral distinction to their decisions. The morality is seen in the individual actions, not the anonymous mass of the Collective, and can only be measured by acts of volition, as acts of compulsion are done to avoid punishment. So only one who is methodological with their individualism, and only acts by volition can have any claim to moral justification, furthermore, any that praise the collective mentality or compulsory indebtedness automatically mark themselves as amoral.

# Liberal vs. Conservative, the play on words to enslave a nation, Part 4

## 1    The New Face of Statism

We are witnessing a new Statism on the rise, the American variety, and in true American tradition, it is a melting pot of other varieties past and present.  It has become a blatant statement in the past two decades, but this is a long running theme of American politics, larger government.  There are many whom argue the case for the government, whom argue that the government is necessary, and it must have some girth in order to be effective.  These are the arguments that create the liberty vs. security debate in all orders and functions, as giving leeway to size in government is a form of security and always comes as a price to the liberty of the people.  To further elaborate, let us take a look at who is arguing this case, the majority of the government is not fighting over liberty vs. security, but rather over what form the security takes.  The government leaves the debate to the people, in order to polarize them, so their creeping assault on the liberty can continue swaying from social to enforcement security.  I intend to show the debate as the people see it, as the government sees it, and how it truly is, furthermore provide the basis of the argument for my new Statist regime theory.

Ben Franklin understood the dangers in the Constitution he took part in, he had made such public by his quote, *"A republic, madam, if you can keep it."*[31] He knew full well, those who were sworn to protect it would attack the republic outlined in the Constitution, and it was the people who would have to maintain it. With this inherent flaw from the beginning, our founders believed the goodness of men would persevere over the will of the elected officials, and though many tried, the force given to the republic was found to be too much. Alas, hindsight is 20/20, and so, we are left with picking up the pieces of centuries of a failed experiment in liberty, beset on two fronts, by government and those that support it blindly.

## 2     A little from the left, a little from the right

The real question that should be burning in the forefront in your mind is, "What is this new Statism?" It is not so easy to explain, though it is a simplistic concept, I am certain that the evidence of this phenomenon cannot elude

---

31http://www.goodreads.com/quotes/show/187130

everyone. It is based on the design of Divide and Conquer, that is, divide the people in order to create the regime, with whoever takes office. Take the most sensitive issues of people make them government business and that is it, once the government plays a hand in any sensitive personal issue; it becomes a great debate among the people.

While the people are bickering between each other over the grand debate of what the government solution should be, there is always a small faction of people; i.e. these are rational people, who state the government is not the answer. These people, wholly committed to the liberty side of the debate are usually ignored, painted as enemies of both right and left (I have personal experience in this). The majority of the people, in contrast, passionately debate what government solution is best, how the government can intervene in the personal lives of the people to make the situation better. This is the cue for the politicians, where to line up in the debate, and as right and left take sides, the majority has already spoken, more government is the answer.

This new Statism falls between communism and fascism; it has the collective tone of shared responsibility and duty to the less fortunate along with the nationalist tone of superiority. One need only look at the actions of the presidents in the last two decades to see a blurring of the lines between left and right, tax and spend republicans along with corporatist democrats, all justifying their positions by the talking points proper to their factions. What the majority of people do not realize is the only progression the government takes in these issues is the enlargement of the government itself, these politicians are wholly committed to the security portion of the debate, and not to liberty. The answer from the government is the positive obligation on the people to give up property for the needs of others: this is welfare.

I will coin a term, Welfarism, to describe what this new Statism is, because that is its main feature, welfare, or the creation of a welfare state. I know many assign this tag to the left wing of politics, but I assure you, it is prevalent on both ends of the political spectrum. Welfare is a security issue, it is the obligation of the people to pay for the security of all others, be it financial or physical, and this is an important factor of welfare, it is not only securing the finances, it is securing the persons. Welfare is every aspect of government action and every aspect of government expansionism; it is providing something for people that they cannot provide for themselves.

This is best understood when one understands the nature of government, that is, what government does naturally, it makes itself necessary and in this necessity it allows the excesses which create the welfare state. Have no illusion; the military, police and all other enforcement services are just as much welfare as entitlement checks, free health care and all social benefits. If one looks at the left arguments for social welfare and follows them to the cause, one will find that government intervention in business is championed by the left under "worker's rights" and "equality". Just as when one examines the right arguments for enforcement welfare and follows them to the cause, one finds government intervention on the private individual is championed by the right under "morality" and "patriotism".

Welfarism, in total, is a theory of positive obligation, using the state as the holder of positive rights in the name of the majority; it is the inherent tyranny of democracy, in the name of the majority the government dictates the lives of others. The focus of the obligation varies, but it is present in all forms of government, that is left, right and current "mainstream" Libertarianism. The left supposes that you have to give up something for the benefit of others in the process of taxation for social benefit, the right for enforcement protection, and "mainstream" Libertarianism (in an insidious variation of this ideology) obligate people to babysit government in order to maintain the liberty they espouse. As plainly as can be put, all factors of any government in America are inherently linked to this ideology of Welfarism, that is, they imply a positive obligation on the people, i.e. giving up liberty, In exchange for a degree of security.

# 3    The People's Case

The people are led by their noses, there are no nice ways to put it, most of the people are being fooled most of the time, and those who know it are the ones that are closer to rational thought.  The people are at each other's throats for issues that are not anyone's business other than people in the situation at the point in time.  This is not an accident; this is planned entirely by the government and executed flawlessly by the mainstream media.  My hope is that people will read this and understand that it is integrity, not compromise, which will solve this issue, that is, integrity on the principle of liberty, with uncompromising fervor, being a freedom extremist.

All issues that the people argue over are easily given collective values, this is by design: categorically leftist's issues are held by a supermajority of the left, as are the right and the modern libertarian.  These issues are what government ought to do, or ought to be allowed to do, that is, what degree of freedom must the people relinquish in the name of the authority and the public debate is never for a true retraction of government, just for adding more law to a weighty legal system.  The most passionate arguments over government policy are rarely that the government should not be granted any positive right, but rather where that positive right lies, what level of security Is the proper tradeoff for what degree of liberty.

Our media structure cradles this argument, as a never-ending battle between the people, either side of the debate is championed as fighting the good fight or whatever, despite the fact that they are both only arguing which chains are more comfortable for them. Pundits and editorial writers rally the people on their heads, specifically to cause conflict, all the time knowing that they are manipulating the masses, doing so with either the demand, or at least appreciation, of the government. These same media focuses are rallied in whole against anyone that speaks in the name of the liberty side of the debate, labeling them as kooks, in a mass movement to discredit.

## 4    The State's Case

The government categorically does not argue on the liberty side of the debates, lest it has people among its own membership that are tolerated and ignored, because this would be an admission on the lack of necessity of the state. If liberty were proper to any form of government, it would automatically cease to be government, as then all aspects of said government could be reasoned away, this is why security through positive obligation is the mantra of politicians.

Major politicians are locked in a debate, but it is a one sided fight, focused on the methodology and execution of security, they assert the liberty is automatically traded off for; this is why you will never hear them ask, "Why are the people giving up this liberty?" Even if one did, there would be either no answer, or one of the major catch phrases, "Public Welfare", or "National Security". They argue for the destiny of stolen money, but rarely do any of us hear the beacon of reason, "It is stealing", they argue what the people ought to conform to, and again rarely do we hear the voice of reason proclaiming the individual's rights. The reasoning behind this, if it is not obvious by now, is the expansion of government; one cannot deny this synthetic a posteriori statement as the act of giving responsibility to the government detracts from the responsibility of the people, in all aspects of the great debate.

## 5 Let Reason Take the Stand

I say "rarely" when I talk of dissent to government within government, because some are there in half spirit, they do not look to categorically deny government, but they seek to lessen the chains. This is still wrong, as it still justifies a positive obligation on the people to support a government in some degree, but the idea is that the less support needed is less Welfarism. If reason in total were to be the guide for these people in government, they would be left without a career, as they would no longer support any form of Statism.

If we use logic and reason, we can see the most heinous faces of Welfarism, we can see the justification of violating rights through positive obligation and we can see the atrocious behavior that Welfarism allows. To understand this, the idea of negative obligation and positive obligation needs to be defined in very plain terms. A negative obligation is when a person is obliged (committed) to not do an action; this is best exemplified by noting that theft is a negative obligation (you are obliged to not steal), as is murder and all other violations of other people. This notion stipulates that people have the general acceptance that self-ownership is the prime tenant of a free society, that one is not the charge of another, but of oneself. In contrast, positive obligation is when one is obliged to do something, not to be confused with a contract, there is no positive obligation to fulfill contracts one enters this is a negative obligation binding the contracted voluntarily and explicitly. In absence of a contract is where societal positive obligation comes in, where the coercion of that society is what enforces the obligation, in other words, when the government has the positive right (more rights) over the individuals.

By no order of logic and reason is positive obligation an acceptable state without explicit consent, now there are those that claim implied consent is sufficient, but implicit consent requires an option away from the obligatory system. Since there is no such pathway that maintains ones property, implicit consent does not stand, since there is no physical contract signed by "the people" individually, explicit consent is impossible.

Consent of the governed has been the long mantra of central government; it must be consented, since we are a government of the people, chosen by the people, in service for the people. What of the people who do not consent, where are they represented, one cannot argue that the chance for representation is a suitable substitution; ought they to be allowed to depart the ties to the government if such a case of non consent were to arise? Is not self-determination a right of man; are you not in possession of the right to provide your food and shelter, without using coercion, and to not be taxed as if it were a privilege?

Using logic and reason, we can easily understand that with or without government, man has the right to provide for his wants, without such a government he is free to act on his environment, with it he has the positive obligation to pay a third party. Whether you consent to the government or not, the basic desires of man: food, shelter, etc., are all taxed, and therefore are all subject to control. We can easily reason the extrapolation, if the government wants you to have a smaller (land) property all it has to do is increase the property tax burden. It can do the same with foods, energy, clothing, where does it end? Logically, it never ends while government is present, it all leads to Welfarism in one form or another and the government takes this money and uses it in order to increase its perceived necessity, fueling the vicious cycle.

## The Final Conclusion

Throughout this very long journey I have highlighted what is wrong with America, what happened to the experiment that drove it to ultimate failure and evolved to a course of action; in the term of these writings on what ought to be done in reaction.  This idea is not popular, made so by the indoctrination of government, but I think it is gaining understanding from individuals who are witnessing the trends, they are seeing the ultimate failure, and addressing it in rethinking their philosophy.

The only answer, in the face of the 231 years of an experiment that resulted in the same oppressive government that the colonists fought to free themselves from is to come to the undeniable conclusion that government and liberty are irreconcilable.  There is a choice to be made: freedom or government, both is not an option, because with government in operation, freedom is always at risk.  We cannot in good conscience expect that a positive obligation to watch government be placed on the whole of the people, we would be hypocritical to do so, confining them to a slavery, and risking that the whim of the majority would put us right back where we are now.

I offer freedom, nothing more, and I stand across from a tide of millions that do not want it, who would rather trade it off than be responsible for their own choices. I offer you the option to associate with whom you choose under agreements you forge and are fully aware of the obligations you place upon yourself. I offer you the only way where a third party does not influence your interactions with others, where all your choices are made by subjective value assessments and are not garnished by illegitimate authority.

You can take my offer, and exert your right to self-determination, or you can go back to sleep, I think you can reasonably deduce what the majority would want of you, what the government would want of you. What you do from this point on, tells the tale of what you want of you.

---

# The Same Coin, Just Different Sides

## Heads I win!

Slavery is an institution of forced labor, the basic needs are met in order to preserve life, but beyond such is a rarity. The slave lives as a captive; a prisoner of circumstance, overseers or taskmasters are the guards of these perpetual prisons. Given the ultimate authority over slaves, the owners (masters) and guards are legally allowed, often encouraged, to treat them as property. To maim rape or kill a slave at whim is a constant possibility as a slave's life and body is not the possession of the slave; it was bought, traded or won in combat. They use force, the lash, to encourage productivity, and in the event of escape they hunt the slave down like a wild animal. The conditions of slave labor, being poor at best are useful in producing one thing less productive work, therefore the slave seeing no real improvement for achievement only seeks to achieve one thing, lower expectations. As a self-pitying victim of circumstance the only realistic rebellion the slave can perform and enjoy is to strain a little less in the field, just enough to feel it, not enough for the guard to notice it and thus avoid the lash. This gradual declination of productivity often inspires others along the same route and slavery becomes a self-defeating institution, not productive enough to maintain itself, let alone the lifestyle of the owner. As the slaves notice another producing less, they in turn fight for the role of the one that is accepted as the least productive by the guards, in the meager hope that the guards will assign lighter work for them to be less productive at or just be tolerated by them as unproductive.

As a slave one's basic needs are met, meagerly at best but met none the less, however there is a price to pay for this which I call the "rewards of slavery", I personally like the irony and after the proper conditioning, it is the slave's consensus. Entertainment is allowed, often encouraged for a happy slave is an obedient one, but only with the fellow slaves and never at any labor hours. Granted the scraps of food not ingested by the owner, consisting of foods not usually considered for eating by the owner or guards make for a veritable concoction of food. As seen in the United States, this is what "soul food" was derived from; one would think that after so many years that the people would reject this food, but it seems the attitude of the slave still exists today. Clothing was provided, often a one size fits all affair, quality is not meant for slaves, so old torn clothing was normally reserved for a slave otherwise it was a mass produced garment, meant only to cover nudity. The owners, out of interest to protect their investment, will also shelter the slaves, ranging from cloth tents to shacks more suited for chicken coops, packing as many as possible per residence. These are the "rewards of slavery" and one must then consider the price of this slavery, what is it that must be given for this, what is the value one would be expected to give for these living conditions? Every moment a slave is alive, he lives his life for another's whim, every ounce of his labor is his owner's profit, and every breath he take is taken mischievously from his owner's pool of fresh air. In return for obedience a slave are kept unarmed, unable to defend himself from other slaves, although more importantly the lash of authority, as a slave that can defend himself is usually not long for this world. The slave trades his children as well, many times slaves were encouraged to copulate, to bring forth a new generation, more obedient and unquestioning, never knowing freedom, never knowing life without the lash.

## Tails you Lose

The prime tenant in Communism as well as its precursor, Socialism, is the individual's life belongs to the collective, that is to say; his livelihood (labor), his private life (free time and family) and all of his property are not his own. The collective is represented by the government in every practical application of these policies, as property holder and arbiter, for the greater (common, public) good. This gives the power of moral sanction to the government to do what it pleases with said life of the individual, so the government can give and take away anything in the name of the nebulous "greater good". The government becomes the owner of the individual, exerting the authority of the "greater good" that outweighs the individuals, in essence using the individual as the means to the government's ends. Government authorities are given full sanction to do as they please with individuals, authorities are often encouraged to treat them as subordinates and subjects were treated in the past, where the authorities badge is a coat of arms that relegates the power of medieval aristocracy. This leads to the annihilation of the individual, as he is then a part of the collective, and as his effort is the property of the government he often begins to prove inability as a goal. The government, with economic authority, will prevent a person from not being able to draw a paycheck, despite the fact that the person does not deserve one. As other members of the collective see the less productive retain their employment they join in the ranks for a competition of inability, the mentality that the quality and quantity of work should suffer so that one is making the most for what labor one produces. If the individual rebel, often the punishment is either death outright or even worse life in a forced labor camp, which is the same as slavery listed above.

The rewards to the collective are promising to the ideal but depressing to the practice, for giving up individuality, and thus freedom, one must really consider the trappings one receives. The individual's needs are met, all be it in regard to what the collective (the government) decides what the needs are, this includes in the most orthodox form everything from housing to every bite of food ingested. Less orthodox forms still exert the same control however they give the illusion of choice by allowing the individual to have money to spend, but regulate and legislate all products and services available to him to exert every bit of control. Entertainment is encouraged in the form of government regulated propaganda, mandatory "volunteerism" and government controlled gatherings, in order to impress conformity and dilute the ability of the individual to break away from the collective: a busy individual is too indoctrinated to be an individual. The services provided are many fold, but it is the quality and the quantity of these services that suffer in these systems, this is not only a function of resources but a function of work ethic as described above, the inefficiency extends to a full transformation of the individual to moral bankruptcy, as they vie for basic comforts. All services provided are availability based as the system is "supposedly" egalitarian, but as resources and poor productivity take their toll as well as rampant theft for sale or trade in the black market, these services are lacking as a rule. Housing is often limited in the most orthodox cases, multiple generations of family living within the same quarters, waiting for the list, which is biased to government favoritism, to grant adult children a separate residence from parents, either way this is not the person's property, rather he is eternally paying the government rent.  Food is rationed, and that was not all, waiting on lines for this food was a regular occupation for many family members that were not working, but all resources were rationed in this manner, from gasoline to electricity and heat.  Clothing is one size fits all (pretty much) and quite uniform, from underwear to coats, the government mass produces garments for distribution, to meet demand, which is impossible to meet and this is the same with all products.  A dominant theme in communism is the defenselessness of the individual, as required by the government, in the name of the "greater good", as the individual is not a factor against the collective.  This is key to this system as it curtails any real potential revolt, and thus leaves the collective as subjects to the government who is the only owner of arms.  Further, all children are required to participate in indoctrination organizations, these organizations starting as early as 3 years old that span until old age, constantly enforcing standardization to conform to the collective, raising children to be good communist soldiers.

## So, what is the difference?

Both institutions focus on a detachment of the individual from the person, that is a breaking of the free will of the individual to a heard like mentality of conformist collectivism.  In either situation the complete liberty of the individual is discarded and all production from said individual is not his own, in the most extreme case neither is his life.  Importance is placed on obedience, the moral high ground of the ruling class or owner, the indoctrination of the next generation and the fulfillment of the basic necessities (however scant this may be).  Total control is a feature of both systems, either through the lash; imprisonment or death, only through conformity to the collective and subordination to authority could one hope to avoid these particular punishments.  Life in and of itself in either system was indeed punishment on the daily life of the average individual, due to the poor quality or complete lack of necessities.  The only real difference between slavery and communism that is apparent is that owners in the slavery institution made no allusion to freedom, they were quite clear the slave was property and despite the consequences if caught there is always an escape. However, in communism, the illusion of freedom is open to the collective as the government insidiously takes control of everything, even the mind, and no matter what you do, there is no escape.

# Why I am an Anarchist.

I have met more resistance for being an open anarchist, in criticism and denial of the validity and possibility of anarchy, than for anything else in my life. I have questioned why, and met the same tired arguments, battled them with reason and common sense and for the life of me I cannot wrap my mind around how people do not get it. My lovely wife explains to me that freedom is a state of being, and if one is not of that particular state then there really is no point in arguing with them. The more I interact with these people the more I am tending to agree with her, to let them go about their merry way, being house slaves, and let them pay the consequences for such accordingly. The false logic some people cling to in the face of reason which troubles me the most is that they rely on an assertion to silence the thought of freedom in their mind.

### *People are Evil...*

This argument really gets me, just right between the eyes, they vary in subject but they are all the same, people are so evil that we need "some group of people" to perform said function; and the only way to make sure that they get the right people, we have to be a collective and go through some choosing process, this choosing process is how we pick the few good people from the sea of bad ones. This argument is used to justify monopoly court and police, government in general and a myriad of other tyrannies too numerous to mention, but at the end of the day, it is still as logically ridiculous.

If we are to assume that the entire world's people are evil, how are we to ensure that the people we choose are the good ones, how do we know they do not lie to get in a position of power and then have their way with us? Look at the last president of the US, he was elected on a platform of no nation building, and what did he do once he had the opportunity to justify it? And if we examine history, this is not a singular case, but rather the norm; it seems that choosing by popular vote yields poor results at best. Maybe this bleak outlook that people are evil is not so much so as it is people who crave power over other people that are evil.

If we are to assume that the entire world's people are evil, why are we still here?  Surely, if you are of one political persuasion, the Soviet Union should have in a fit of evil, nuked the US or came in a red dawn scenario or some other nonsensical plot?  If you are of the other should not the evil capitalists during the Reagan or other like administrations done it to them?  On the local level, one would think if this argument were true, with the increase in police and law crime would drop, but the opposite has actually happened.  Yet again, history shows us that regardless of the opinion that evil people are abound in the world, there is very little evidence to prove this opinion true, at best there are few evil people in the world, most likely few good as well and the vast majority are a sea of sheep following the charismatic shepherd around, giving little thought as to why they do as they do.

I am beginning to believe that the argument that people want to convey with this tactic is in truth, very real, that people in general are sheep, and do not think about what and, more importantly, why they are doing as they are told, they are just going through the motions until they shuffle from the mortal coil.  Without the group in control of them, these people will not act, they will not know what to do and in large part will die, as any animal that has lost all sense of survival.  So the argument then becomes, for the sake of others, those that are not sheep ought to be their slaves, pay for the system that allows them survival.

Basically, what people making this argument are saying is if one is able to live independent of the system the sheep need, one ought to be part of it, that is, sacrifice autonomy for nothing. In reality, "people are evil" is an argument for slavery, meaning the sheep that require enslavement to a state do not want to be alone in slavery, it is them looking to share their misery with their betters.

### *Someone Will Always be in Control*

This argument can be said to be truth in a context, I agree that someone will always be in control, even as an anarchist. There is a primary difference though in the context of the argument and what I mean, that is, whom is in control of what. The argument put to me is really that there will always be a slave master, and if you are not the master, be a good slave and do as you are told, this is not my stance. My thoughts are the individual is either in control, or he chooses slavery, he has the freedom to choose freely between them.

This argument really boils down to the right of ownership of the self, do you own you or does someone else? Posed to me is that people will choose an authority to control them, maybe not consciously to enslave themselves, but rather to enslave others (refer to previous argument), and as such, everyone ought to participate. This is basically the self-defense argument for government that does not prove its authority just; it only proves the government is a coercive device and if you are not a part of you are the victim of.  What they are failing to logically put together is that they are proving why any Statism is wrong, that it is inherently slavery and it does not stand as the best option.

I believe that people ought to be in control of themselves, that their day to day life is their business and not some authority's, that when they enter the market they decide what they want, what they offer and what values they place on these things.  This is someone being in control, it is just, simply because it is the individual being in control of his possessions, be it his body, or his property.  What people who use this argument are really saying is that humans cannot control themselves and need an authority, which leads us to the next argument.

### Civilization requires Government

This is nothing more than the most heinously fallacious argument that can be imagined; it is basically stating that the human condition is so depraved that without someone to force them to be civil, they will destroy one another.  Not only is this showing the world that the person making the argument is basically equating everyone to savage beasts that cannot wait to victimize his fellow man, but also completely disregards the reality of how government came about.  Civil society did not derive from government, rather government is a product of uncivilized people trying to control a civil society, civility cannot be forced and it comes from free interaction in trade. If one owns his property and wants something someone else has, he may interact with this other person in a number of ways. He can trade property the other wants in exchange, offer services for this desired property or he can take it, only one of these is uncivilized, what the person who accepts this argument says is that individuals will opt for the only uncivilized choice. The claim is that it is easier, that it is no loss and that it is effective, none of this is true. It is not easier, at no loss or effective because of retaliation, if you trade for something you are not investing time, energy and resources to dissuade or react to retaliation. Not to mention that it is not effective because you do not know for certain that you will succeed, so the investment made to do the act of taking over trading may produce no results. But with all of this logic stacked against this argument, people insist that the choice will be to be uncivilized.

Civil society was derived from interaction between humans, in absence of any authority, by simply choosing to trade over take, if this never happened we would never have had any society to begin with. Claiming that government produced civil society is not only wrong, but also quite dumb, it is like saying that one man was civil among a group of savages and he forced them to be civil. How this makes sense is beyond me, the reality is that people civilized naturally, by finding that trade was preferable to taking, it is effective, it requires only the work to acquire the desired property and the individual makes the subjective decision on the value he is willing to trade for the property. Then came government, when uncivilized people decided that if given authority they could take with less risk. They gathered other uncivilized people and forced government on civilized people, therefore through coercion of civilized people was government born, not the other way around. Evidence of this is seen all throughout history, as governments cast tyranny after tyranny on civilized people time and time again; every war, every genocide, are all products of government. As a matter of fact government cannot help itself but show what it really is, all it takes is time.

## Monopolies and Cartels and Trusts, Oh my!

If there was ever the biggest lie we have been taught in schools it is that there have been big business interests that completely dominated the market when the market was "freer" in the United States. The real economic history has been revised to make laissez faire seem as if the rich will take all control and enslave the people, when quite frankly the opposite occurred in reality. The myth that the Sherman Act was used prior to Theodore Roosevelt to protect the people from these big business interests is propaganda to the tune of what the Soviet citizens were inundated with about America and Capitalists alike. The truth is far less convincing that the free market produces predatory monopolies, and in fact, the predatory monopolies could not have existed without the assistance of the government to secure.

Every industry it was tried in, in the less regulated market, the monopoly, cartel or trust, at gaining monopolistic status, that is 60% or better, and they had gone about cutting production and raising prices, the opposite of what we were taught happened, time and time again.  There was no mighty tycoon crushing the masses, withholding a standard of living from people because of their intolerable greed, when the monopoly set up was achieved, and the production cut and price raise was applied, people freely entered into the market against the monopoly.  In fact, most monopoly corporations, without state intervention, failed because of this truth, the free market will always tend towards the true market value.  If ones firm wishes to artificially inflate the market value for his commodity, he will be out competed by new firms in a free market, i.e. one that allows for free entry into it.  The only thing that allows a monopoly to remain after it has formed is the government, through tariffs, licensing, regulations and such.  The government, through willful action or ignorance, is the sole reason monopolies persist, and that the government education system teaches the opposite is telling that it is more willful and less ignorance.

In short, the government mandate riddled, regulated market is the predatory market that fosters monopolies and causes untold suffering on the general population, this is the opposite of what the government would like you to know to be the truth, but the real truth prevails.

### *The Question of Liberty*

It is said that the "proper role" of government is to protect the rights of the citizens, it is a nice story, but the reality of the situation is quite the opposite. Even the founders of the US Constitution believed in majority that the government is not the protector of the rights of the people. The basic language of the Declaration of Independence suggests, but not demands, that a government would be formed to replace the original government, which would be disposed of, and so on if the replacement turned out to be another tyranny. In fact, Jefferson, in the Declaration, in his use of language basically claims that treason is not a crime, but rather the right of the individual to break ties with a tyranny that has become oppressive, inherently tied to the right of secession. This is one of the reasons why Jefferson said there should be a rebellion every 20 years:

"God forbid we should ever be twenty years without such a rebellion. The people cannot be all, and always, well informed. The part, which is wrong, will be discontented, in proportion to the importance of the facts they misconceive. If they remain quiet under such misconceptions, it is lethargy, the forerunner of death to the public liberty."

~Thomas Jefferson

A wise man once said:

"Those who would give up essential liberty to purchase a little temporary safety deserve neither liberty nor safety."

~Benjamin Franklin

The trade off for any security is always liberty, I would even hazard to say the personal security that one would have in absence of government would be paid by some liberty in a sense. The difference being of course that when I actively secure my home, the liberty I trade is the liberty to do things that do not involve my security. For example, if I contract a service from others, the resources used to pay for those services are not at my liberty to dispense in other projects, or if I chose to provide for my own defense alone, the time and effort cannot be used elsewhere while employed on my security. When one uses government to take this role, history proves the Franklin quote true, what liberties have we relinquished to the government already for minor security bonuses? Financial liberty has been attacked to pay for foreign wars, a bloated military and interventionist policies. Privacy has been destroyed in National Security interests, not to mention Speech, Press,

Religion, Petition, Property, and Due Process. Using the argument that the US has not had a terror attack on our soil in the past X years is made of rice paper, rather than being attacked here we are sending people to the middle east, basically saying those who fight in this war do not count as they are subject to a world of car bombs and ambush attacks. Most often the people applauding the lives of our soldiers are inadvertently saying they are worth less than the average citizen as they are pushed into mandatory suicide.

The blatant lie of the concept of rights protector is so obvious it boggles the mind that the masses believe it is true, simply because they have no coherent understanding of what liberty actually is. Orwell's statement in *1984* "Freedom is Slavery" is quite honestly the only way someone can rationalize the idea that the government protects their rights; it is as oxymoronic as the Orwellian quote. When one looks at the reality of what government does, all law is a rights violation on behalf of the state on its population: even laws that would exist without the state are inherently a rights violation because the state has no authority to make any laws dictating the behavior of individuals. Laws that dictate what an individual does with their own body, property or what an individual can own as property, can only be seen as rights violations, it implies that the individual's body and property is in part automatically under the control of the state. So the idea that the state protects rights falls apart once the state passes a law that gives itself access to the individual's private property, one could go on with the reasoning that private property does not exist within a government controlled area.

## *Tell Me What the Free Market Anarchist Society Will Be Like....*

It is amazing how people really do not understand what a free market is, we have a regulated market in the United States, it always has been the case, the Constitution allows for it at the hands of Congress. No one can tell you what a free market anything will be like, it is not like what we have today, that is the best I, or anyone else that understands the free market system, can tell you. I can give predictions on likely possibilities, but it is impossible to predict real free market results, as they are based on individual actions, and as such are based on the choices of individuals, which are wholly subjective.

Let us start with the daunting task of a potential prediction in the field of the market itself, right at its heart, money. Free market money is one of the taboo topics of statists mainly because when you control the money in creation and use, you control the people. Free market money would mean basically that the media of exchange would be created privately, this could be in any form, paper, metallic coin, etc, and the value would be chiefly maintained by the producers of such. The reason I default to a money system and not barter is because the money system has portability and storage benefits that are highly efficient. It is the profit motive that stabilizes the money, which a private creator produces, because if his money is unstable, people will opt to not use it, remember I am talking about an anarchist society, so there is no government to coerce the people to use it. Also in the free market scenario there is the availability to compete in this business so it cannot be assumed that there will be a monopoly dominating money creation.

In dealing with a medium of exchange, that is, money, most people have the argument that you cannot have money without the government, that there must be some authority to regulate it. This fallacious notion comes from a thought that the government has a role in the economy of an overseer of sorts, that without the "master" the slaves will run amok is more realistic to the representation of this argument. The economic position of government is to be a consumer, not a regulator, not a producer but only a consumer, it consumes goods and in the usual case it undermines the market by allocation (legal theft) rather than purchase. The market is controlled by people who produce goods and services and those who consume these goods and services by purchase; a common mugger helps the economy as much as the government can in this respect. The only visible end of the government in the market is coercion, seizure of assets through taxation (or one is imprisoned), regulation (or one is fined/imprisoned) and/or manipulation of the money supply (based on a false authority). So why is the production of a medium of exchange supposed to be different, why would we assume that money is where the government is honest, when it is dishonest everywhere else, why is it that we assume that government can defy economic science and have a neutral or positive effect on the economy? Furthermore, placing the medium of exchange in the hands of a private enterprise means that there is a vested interest in sustaining a stable value to the currency, which is retaining the utility of their product. Hayek proposes in *A Free Market Monetary System*:

"I think it is entirely possible for private enterprise to issue a token money which the public will learn to expect to preserve its value, provided both the issuer and the public understand that the demand for this money will depend on the issuer being forced to keep its value constant; because if he did not do so, the people would at once cease to use his money and shift to some other kind."[32]

I have to agree with Hayek, the private business has more at stake to retain a stable value of the currency it issues

---

32  http://www.mises.org/story/3204

than a government does, historically we have seen the manipulation of money with no alternative have drastic effects on the people of a given nation, any of the hyperinflation incidents of the 20th century can tell us that.

Classically people default to police and courts as another reason we need government, but I really do not see how one requires the other, in a free market scenario, police would most likely be made possible by private business, as well as court. Again the profit motive would protect the consumer, since the consumer is not required to subscribe to a particular service, each will look to provide the best service for the least cost. One may attack this scenario as slighted to the rich, but in reality, more purchase power is in the hands of all but the rich. Asset ownership is what makes the wealthy actually wealthy, this is not liquid asset, but rather other property, and as such is not useful for immediate usage.

Another popular attack is that they would make war between themselves, and again this is destroyed by profit motive. It shows that the price of violence is a concept completely alien to many people who argue against the free market. If you consider the price needed to pay a free individual to risk his life, the costs in benefits if he does die, resources allocated to ensure victory and dissuade retaliation as compared to a protection company that would not choose such Viking-like measures, the market logic presents itself.  Paying a business that defaults to making "war" over peaceably solving issues will cost more, and as such will not be attractive to most subscribers, this is not to say these businesses will not exist, but will not be the norm, and more than not will fail to be successful in retaining clientele or employees.  As Murray Rothbard suggests in *For a New Liberty: A Libertarian Manifesto*:

"To assume that police would continually clash and battle with each other is absurd, for it ignores the devastating effect that this chaotic "anarchy" would have on the business of all the police companies. To put it bluntly, such wars and conflicts would be bad — very bad — for business. Therefore, on the free market, the police agencies would all see to it that there would be no clashes between them, and that all conflicts of opinion would be ironed out in private courts, decided by private judges or arbitrators."[33]

I am not too sure that violent protection agencies would survive long, possibly at all, on reconsideration, because the ones willing to pay the fees have to have in the back of their heads the consequences of others potentially out bidding them.  Not to mention that if such were the

---

33 http://mises.org/rothbard/newlibertywhole.asp#p215

standard accepted practice, those that could afford the service would not for long, impoverished because they cannot force others to pay for a violent group of thugs through taxation.

And then there is the other troubling thought about police protection, that it is a commodity the government provides to all equally. As Murray Rothbard poses in *For a New Liberty: A Libertarian Manifesto*:

"In the first place, there is a common fallacy, held even by most advocates of laissez-faire, that the government must supply "police protection," as if police protection were a single, absolute entity, a fixed quantity of something which the government supplies to all. But in actual fact there is no absolute commodity called "police protection" any more than there is an absolute single commodity called "food" or "shelter." It is true that everyone pays taxes for a seemingly fixed quantity of protection, but this is a myth."[34]

The train of thought behind the need for police protection, or a military for that matter, justifies the State to provide food and shelter to all for paying taxes as well, as these are

---

34 http://mises.org/rothbard/newlibertywhole.asp#p215

"needed", much in the way people stand on police protection. How does one on the "right" disambiguate police from the entitlement mentality they associate checks, food and shelter, one would think, if we boil away all the jargon, are they not the same? The myth about the difference in what is known as welfare in the United States and police protection is simply that, a myth, if you justify the State in taking taxes for police protection you justify the State doing the same for all "Welfare" programs.

### *In Conclusion*

Philosophically and economically the state is unjustifiable, so the only alternative is anarchism, which is, existence without the state. There is no reason for the existence of the state aside from the usefulness of the state to those who would steal from others in the populace, it is fundamentally an organization meant to minimize the threat of punishment for theft. Civilized people do not require a state to keep other civilized people from violating their rights; rather uncivilized unsuccessful people need a state to be predatory on other people in order to mitigate the costs of their failures. No one can rationally argue that the state is beneficial to anyone without first violating the rights of others, and the claim that this is the price of liberty is not only erroneous, but a malicious lie propagated by the state. Nothing can defend the position of the state without first admitting that the defender is in fact a beneficiary of the state and the root cause of the defense is in fact the desire to benefit off the backs of other people.

The state does not and cannot defend individual liberty, which if experience does not make it obvious, the historical reality of law making (specifically in the US) viewed through epistemic examination amply proves. Law making, inherently, even when the law is relatively just, is a rights violation simply because it is surrendering to non-consented authority. For one to epistemologically justify the state, which could only be done by an individual consenting to every action the state takes, still only justifies it on an individual basis. This combined with majority prevailing on each vote, to elect representatives and to pass laws, creates an atmosphere where unanimous consent is impossible. If, in the US, we are to adhere to the philosophical basis of the American Revolution, since consent is impossible to prove on a mass scale, any government derived will be non-consented and therefore unjust. So, on a philosophical basis, only autonomy (Self Government) is just simply because it is the only way to have unanimous consent.

The state is not economically beneficial, rather it is disadvantageous, it violates market logic, and not only in its existence, but also in every action it takes. It acts as a monopolist does: it creates false scarcity, it dictates price and it is a predatory market presence. It uses the aforementioned unjust authority in order to maintain its monopoly status in the economy, and as history shows us, unjust authority is the only maintainer of its monopoly status. The insanity continues when the state's actions cumulate to foster private monopolies, this is how they reinforce their own monopoly status over the economy, basically by causing a problem and then promoting more economic control as the solution.

In short there is no durable benefit on the individual basis that the government provides, in the long run, there is no benefit at all, in contrast to the free market. The free market and the capitalist system of ownership, existing in a society of autonomous individuals are the only reasonable path to durable benefit, in short and long term. When one examines the prospect of individual liberty, capitalist ownership is how it is realized in reality, and the same holds true for economic prosperity and the free market. As our inherent right to own ourselves, which is to not be slaves, is present only in capitalism, the free market is the only way to interact in capitalism and the only way for a free market to exist is in absence of government, therefore anarchy is the only option remaining.

I am an anarchist because the control to our lives, liberty and property are paramount, and only realized in an anarchic capitalist setting.

# Libertarianism: The Natural Phenomenon

The philosophy of Libertarianism is the school of thought devoted to individual liberty, where the individual has supreme authority over his own life in all respects. It asserts that freedom is natural for man, that is, it is as much of man's nature to be free as it is for him to breathe. This is the core belief of the philosophy, every great libertarian thinker has come to the same conclusion: anarchism or stateless society, free markets combined with capitalism or the individual right of property ownership as the ultimate libertarian goal. The comparative results of logical deduction are not coincidental, each reasoning the state as the ultimate aggressor, and freedom as it is inherent to men does not require a state, rather it requires the lack of such.

### *Man's Nature*

The nature of man is suspect to say the least, as each man is the observer of this phenomenon, if we base it on recorded history, more men have been enslaved than free, but does this denote what is in man's nature? I think not, Seneca the younger, around the 3rd Century B.C. wrote:

"It is a mistake to imagine that slavery pervades a man's whole being; the better part of him is exempt from It: the body indeed is subjected and in the power of a master, but the mind is independent, and indeed is so free and wild, that it cannot be restrained even by this prison of the body, wherein it is confined, from following its own impulses, dealing with gigantic designs, and soaring into the infinite, accompanied by all the host of heaven."[35]

The Stoics had observed that the body can be put in slavery, but the mind would always remain free, or external conditions juxtaposed on internal freedom, the stoics referred to this as sui juris, freedom of the soul. It is obvious that internally, no one can coerce a man to believe anything he chooses not to, it is an exercise in futility, there is no way to prove success, all you can do is coerce his external actions, but his mind is verily immune from detection.

If slavery were the nature of man, then freedom would be the anomaly, time would have started with man in absolute authority, the stricter and more absolute would produce less resistance to the authority than more. This idea that slavery is the natural state of man presupposes that it is the ideal state of man and he ought to be enslaved. When we study all things in nature, animate and inanimate we observe them and their reaction to their environments. In

---

[35] http://evans-experientialism.freewebspace.com/seneca02.htm Section XX

the ideal environment the inanimate endures time and the animate thrives, the Pyramids are in an ideal environment for their existence to endure time, the Golden Gate Bridge however is not. The Pyramids of Egypt have stood millennia without repair; the Golden Gate Bridge requires continuous repair and refinishing in order to endure its environment. Tropical animals in the tropics, if left to contend with nature, thrive, but place them in the arctic and they perish. Similarly if we look at man in slavery and compare him with one who is not, which progresses his situation, advances his life, innovates his works, and reproduces, out of the two which is the one that thrives? It is obvious the slave does nothing but toil at his master's whim, he is a slave and remains as such, he does not innovate as he only benefits his master, he does not reproduce often, more than likely unwilling to subject his offspring to enslavement. A side note, if the slaves at any time in history were willing to reproduce, would the "legal" slave trade have continued until the 1800's, evidence points to unwillingness. The man who is not a slave benefits from progressing, advancing, and innovating, as such he is eager to engage in these activities, eager to bring offspring in the world. Which would you consider thriving? A man who is treated as a mere beast of burden, even in the best of cases, is still a man without any surety of the next moment of his life; he has no personal stake in his future and thus no impetus to thrive. Conversely the man who is free has his entire future at his hands, he is the sole steward of it, and as such he is sure to make the best attempt to expand his future horizons, hence he is driven by invested interest, or if you rather personal stake, to thrive. Simply put, a slave lives in a state of inescapable stagnation and a free man lives in a state of potential flourish, this does not denote the free man's life is perfect, just that he has authority to strive for perfection within his life. Furthermore it is noted a man's nature is predisposed to be free and any state of being un-free is, therefore, unnatural to him.

### Man in a State

I am not oblivious to the apparent contradiction of the day, people seem to be stagnating despite having freedom, in fact they are acting more and more like slaves as time progresses would this not point to the opposite solution to the hypothesis of man's nature? No, it does not, the contradiction of the time is not that free men are acting the opposite of the way they ought to act there is no contradiction as they are not free to begin with. This may come as a shock to some; this may just be rehashing attained knowledge for others, those that it is common knowledge for, I implore, bear with me for the sake of those who require this knowledge they do not already have.

Man currently exists wholly within a state, that is, there is no man living on earth not existing under some form of government or another, some more privileged than others, some less oppressed than others, but all have a governing body ruling them. The State can be defined as a group of individuals with positive rights over the constituency of a general geographical area determined by their ability to exert coercion on said constituency. Positive rights is the authority to take action superseding the rights of another, such as the authority to tax, which would be called theft without this "right". All one can say about the constituency of said area is that they participate in the State in a vain attempt to avoid the coercion that is undoubtedly in their future if they do not, as Lysander Spooner remarks in "No Treason: A Constitution of No Authority":

"He sees further, that, if he will but use the ballot himself, he has some chance of relieving himself from this tyranny of others, by subjecting them to his own. In short, he finds himself, without his consent, so situated that, if he use the ballot, he may become a master; if he does not use it, he must become a slave."[36]

Even in the supposed "Land of the Free" men are merely enslaved to all others, they participate in the state function of voting to be their neighbor's master rather than his slave. We have only to examine the 2008 election cycle to

---

36 http://files.meetup.com/1496776/NoTreason.pdf pg.5

understand this, need I remind people of the main impetus of electing the current president, a great many that were publicized in the news, the statements about old white men, the implications of racism, implications that persist today if one dares disagree with the current administration. One should note, however, he is reminded at every election that total oppression is a majority decision against him, so even as the master of his neighbor he remains enslaved to the ballot box.

I regret to inform the unknowing readers, you are indeed not free, you are subject to the state and in their opinion, you have no rights, you have privileges the state may remove at any time. Is it then any wonder why a man living in what is fallaciously referred to as freedom is expressing the traits of a slave? Why not cut to the quick and understand what your nature is telling you all along, this is not how life ought to be, the state is not molding man's nature it is plain that man's nature is rejecting the state.

### Natural Rights

The concept of natural rights simply put is the rights man has in regard to his nature; they are in effect inescapable to man, inalienable as it is stated. How are a man's rights derived, who do they come from, what are they exactly, where are they applicable, when do they have them and why is it so important? All of these questions face the libertarian, and if one is to try to explain Libertarianism, it may behoove one to understand the case for natural rights.

Natural rights are derived from nature, as the name presupposes, the natural state of man is to be alive, man as a creature is not the sum of his parts he is also his mind. The assertion that the natural state of man is to be alive, once we strip the paranormal phenomenon of superstition, is supported by man being more than the sum of his parts. If you take the mind from a man, is he the same, the answer is no, a man in a vegetative state is different from a man intact. He is physically still the same, he breathes, eats, etc, but his persona is changed, his mind has lost something beyond the physical embodiment of a man. According to Aristotle, man is a rational animal, meaning that he has an ability which makes him unique, he has reason and this phenomenon is the examination that there is something more to man than a collection of chemical material. So, we can assert safely that man is more than his constituent parts, and what makes him more than his parts, his mind, is absent when he is dead, therefore, the natural state of man is to be alive. Thus as he has a right, inherent to his nature, to live he has the right to procure the necessities to live. Primary to this is his body, a man's body is necessary for him to live, and the maintenance of said body ought to be within his rights to provide for. Here we derive property, as the body his mind is attached to is necessary to the existence of it; he has a property right over the body his mind is encapsulated within.

These rights are granted to all men, just for being able to act in their environment, for having the ability to procure the necessities to live, it is natural to men, so the question of who grants these rights is answered with no one. These rights are inherent; they are not subject to confiscation by any external authority, only an individual can consent to curb his rights and his alone.

The natural rights of man are actually a minimal list; they encompass his right to live in liberty and procure the necessities to sustain such a life while retaining total liberty. All rights are in fact able to be filed down to property rights, as man has a right to the property that is his own body, as a self owner he has the right to sustain it; which leads to the conclusion that he also has the right to secure property, as Herbert Spencer states in "The Great Political Superstition":

"Animal life involves waste; waste must be met by repair; repair implies nutrition. Again, nutrition presupposes obtainment of food; food cannot be got without powers of prehension, and, usually, of locomotion; and that these powers may achieve their ends, there must be freedom to move about. If you shut up a mammal in a small space, or tie its limbs together, or take from it the food it has procured, you eventually, by persistence in one or other of these courses, cause its death. Passing a certain point, hindrance to the fulfillment of these requirements is fatal. And all this, which holds of the higher animals at large, of course holds of man."[37]

Humans are animals; first and foremost, albeit we are rational animals, we are still animals none the less and it is foolish to think that the laws of nature do not apply to man.

As all humans have these rights, where is the boundary, where does "A's" rights end and "B's" rights begin? Quite simply at the end of each individual's property, in terms of land it is the property line between the two, in terms of objects it is ownership and in terms of interaction it is in life. Libertarians conceptualize this boundary in the non-aggression principle (NAP), which Walter Block sums up, in "The Non-Aggression Axiom of Libertarianism":

"The non-aggression axiom is the lynchpin of the philosophy of libertarianism. It states, simply, that it shall be legal for anyone to do anything he wants, provided only

---

37http://www.econlib.org/library/LFBooks/Spencer/spnMv S4.html#The%20Great%20Political%20Superstition section 4.38

that he not initiate (or threaten) violence against the person or legitimately owned property of another."[38]

This does beg the question of ownership, how does one state the claim of property ownership, how do we know where A's property ends and B's begins?  Murray Rothbard explains the concept of, and justification for, Homesteading in "The Ethics of Liberty":

"If every man has the right to own his own person and therefore his own labor, and if by extension he owns whatever property he has "created" or gathered out of the previously unused, unowned state of nature, then who has the right to own or control the earth itself? In short, if the gatherer has the right to own the acorns or berries he picks, or the farmer his crop of wheat, who has the right to own the land on which these activities have taken place? Again, the justification for the ownership of ground land is the same for that of any other property. For no man actually ever "creates" matter: what he does is to take nature-given matter and transform it by means of his ideas and labor energy. But this is precisely what the pioneer— the homesteader—does when he clears and uses previously unused virgin land and brings it into his private ownership. The homesteader—just as the sculptor, or miner—has transformed the nature-given soil by his labor

38 http://www.lewrockwell.com/block/block26.html

and his personality. The homesteader is just as much a "producer" as the others, and therefore just as legitimately the owner of his property. As in the case of the sculptor, it is difficult to see the morality of some other group expropriating the product and labor of the homesteader. (And, as in the other cases, the "world communist" solution boils down in practice to a ruling group.) Furthermore, the land communalists, who claim that the entire world population really owns the land in common, run up against the natural fact that before the homesteader, no one really used and controlled, and hence owned the land. The pioneer, or homesteader, is the man who first brings the valueless unused natural objects into production and use."[39]

Beyond the initial ownership of property, after homesteading has taken place, the free market mechanism of title transfer is determinant of the ownership right over any particular property either land or other material object. Title transfer allows, in a free society, for the best claims on property to be respected based on the free exchange of goods and it also provides for reasonable proof of prior ownership in the case of fraud.

At the time when a man is able to provide for his own sustenance he is in full possession of rights, considering

---

39 http://mises.org/rothbard/ethics/eight.asp

infants who are unable to acquire the basic necessities of life are under the guardianship of those who can provide for them do not have full possession of rights. This may sound monstrous, but please bear with the logic before casting judgment on the position of dependents rights. Whereas we witness in nature a child without parenting would surely perish, his inferior capacity to undergo sustaining his life requires a guardian, he has what is termed as having no value. His value to himself would be the ability to provide for him the nourishment, shelter and clothing, of which I am sure, no one can argue an infant is completely incapable of, therefore he cannot be a self owner. I would be remiss if I did not mention that the child does obtain value to himself quite rapidly, far faster than what is commonly considered, and society places arbitrary constraints on the young from being able to realize their true value when they gain it.

The child is homesteaded by a woman when, with the help of a contingent male addition, creates a child, but what is maintained is not ownership, only the right to continue homesteading the child or guardianship. At any time the woman can choose to give up homesteading the child, for lack of a better term abandoning, and in such a case, to be in line with the principle of homesteading she is required to allow egress. I would suggest Dr. Walter Block's "Libertarianism, Positive Obligations and Property Abandonment: Children's Rights" for further, far more detailed reading, I am glazing over the concept. In order to abandon, one is required to make notice of one's intentions, or they are just owners in absentee, in the case of a child, this is murder, so to be consistent with Libertarian principle, absentee ownership of homesteading rights of a child are not possible. This would also mean they could not forestall, or blockade said child, for in order to do such would disallow others to homestead the child and lead again to murder. What I mean by egress is that the parents of said child are obligated to allow others to take on the responsibility of homesteading the child, by adoption (free or pecuniary), or by allowing others to take ownership of the homesteading rights. Understandably, abandonment of a child while in the womb is not conducive to allowing egress, but in this case it is literally impossible to allow homesteading rights to another as the child is unable to exist outside the womb for a time. As such while a woman is carrying a child it is a part of her body, and just as she has total rights over her body, she has total rights over the contents there of, and may choose to abort said pregnancy.

In short, the child has a right to expect the benefits of guardianship, reasonable food, shelter and clothing, until, and only until, he has the value in order to provide for himself. This is when the rights of guardianship expire and he attains full rights unto himself, this is particularly when he becomes a self owner.

Why are natural rights important, often the crux of the matter is always the why, I would think it obvious that natural rights are integral to civilized society. It is apparent that people can exist without government; there was a time before government, and many societies had existed throughout time which never acquired one. These societies were not barbarous savages raping and pillaging across the world, oddly enough, this type of savagery was delegated to those with governments. Conversely, these societies had and respected common rules about violating others, in person or property, and existed in a state of internal peace. The only explanation of these events is that natural rights of man are a very real part of the human animal, an integral part of the nature of man, and not only existent without government but man thrives with it. It is government which is unnatural for man, an artificial apparatus, coercing him away from his natural state of freedom.

# Afterthoughts

I thought I would give a little closure to this book, not so much a summation of it, rather a declaration that I am not at the end of the learning process, not entirely refined and I am unsure I will ever be completely done. It has been a long year and there are quite potentially many more long years of learning in my future, I truly hope there is, I believe learning is a lifelong process. The radical shift in my understanding in the short term is in reality only the beginning, and I intend to be prolific as I develop in the future. Without further ado, I present my current position.

## State of the Revolution within Me

In the looming disquiet of the state of affairs in my home country, the United States, I am inclined to put forth the options for revolution, why I have chosen the methods I have and why I reject in part or in total others. Revolution does not mean violence, violence is one method, however there is also counter-involvement in the state, educating against the state and operating outside of the state which is commonly referred to as "going Galt". All who have come before me have discussed and advocated options among these, rejected others, as we are all individuals we all have different roads we prefer to reach the destination of Liberty, certainly there is not only one way.

To the neophyte idealistic youth violence is the most direct systematic path to end the state, what is not usually considered by these advocates is the reality of the end results to these means. This is not a subtle means, it requires open organization of military to fight the established state and it leaves out the resulting military potential, if successful, to fill the void where the state once was. Violent revolution is only a means to change the hands of the state from one group to another and as we see in history, at best it is a band-aid on an axe wound, at worst it is a second axe wound all together. I am by no means a pacifist, if violence comes I believe it should be met with violent resistance of a magnitude to cease the violence against oneself, but as a means of meaningful change, it is useless. What I mean by meaningful change is a change in the direction to liberty, the abolition of coercive, violent monopolies and the replacement of these with voluntary human interaction, violence is not a means to these ends.

Counter involvement in the state is taking ones principles to the state through convincing a constituency to elect oneself based on those principles. Once elected within the state the theory is to convince others to "roll back" the state legislatively, basically to use the state to eliminate the state. I used to think this was possible, but history is one hell of a teacher, and adeptly insists otherwise for a very good reason. I failed to recognize Lord Acton's famous statement, which when we examine history proves to be as much an axiom as Mises' "Action Axiom":

"Power corrupts, absolute power corrupts absolutely."

It is for this reason partisanship has never worked to remove prior encroachments of the state, either we are left with a participant in the state, who retains his principle and is a pariah which results nothing or he have a participant who is corrupted and is far more injurious to minimizing the government, as he has a modicum of trust, which he has violated for political gain. This is truth, both historically proven time and time again, logically deduced and it makes evident that limited government is not only unattainable but Utopian. As this book plainly displays I had advocated limited government, and in a way I still do, rather than the ends of a means, it has become for me a means to an end. I would like to see a majority or at least a strong minority faction of the state clinging to principle just to paralyze the state's march to absolutism. Though I know this is a dream more than a tangible goal I still do look to those who would reduce the state, though not abolish it, as fellow travelers who have yet to bring this idea to the logical conclusion. I have in the past, and still do lend intellectual support to individuals whom look to change minds in the direction of minimizing the state as these people do not have the power of the state in their hands. I do not wholly reject counter-involvement in the state but I offer those who partake in this tactic no trust, I scrutinize every action they take and if they fail to live up to the goals they set for themselves I am their most vigorous dissenter.

The scholarly work of educating against the state is a long tradition, rooted in history by great minds and continued today; indeed I intend this book as one such pursuit. One cannot ignore the facts though the practice of education has opened more minds it has not, however brought about an end to statist oppression. Education is a tool, it seeds thought, it develops into knowledge, but knowledge is not power if it is never acted upon and this is the inherent weakness of education alone. Education without action is the trend I notice from a great deal of people around me, it could be from feelings of fear or futility. As I noted earlier, people are more than willing to stand on a street corner and shout, but very few are willing to adapt themselves to a few basic changes which will lead in the direction of change. Education is the groundwork for meaningful change, but is not the actual change it proposes, this requires the actions of individuals to manifest. If we are to imagine liberty as a house, the foundation, framing, plumbing and electrical systems are all education, operating as its structure, conversely the finished product of the house is the result of the action taken guided by this structure. Liberty is a finished product of two factors, education and action, without either one the product fails to be realized; without education the action is unguided and therefore potentially wasted, without action education will produce nothing.

"Going Galt" is a reference to Ayn Rand's book *Atlas Shrugged*; it denotes removing oneself from a society which is no longer serving the basic interests of the individual in question. If you have read this book, and I do recommend it as a good read, most which purport this tactic are falling short on many levels. Rand had proposed a group of people, living completely separate from a failing United States, providing all the amenities of life for their counter society and exchanging them on a free market, using gold coin as their currency. Currently people who seek to fit this mold can be generalized in two groups, people who like this slogan, and Agorists. The people in the first category are much like the people from the above topic of education, ones who say much and do nothing; they seem to me, and this is an opinion, to be looking for a charismatic leader to lead the way to liberty. The major failing of this plan is witnessed by any astute historian; charismatic leaders are often times the most horrendous dictators when given the comparative advantage over the population. The Agorists are however, if acting, very different; they are actively seeking the means to operate a free market in spite of the oppressive state apparatus. As I understand the concept, the agorist seeks to eliminate the state by way of withdrawal, and applying the Konkin idea of counter-economics. In my opinion the agorist philosophy is a bridge between the state regime and the completely Libertarian or anarchist society I advocate.

I applaud the means, it is not initiating violence and it respects individual liberty, but I am unsure there is support of the anarchistic ends I seek, the agorists I encounter in the majority do not *hate the state,* as Murray N. Rothbard put it. Rather they are less unhappy with a state as they are with the current state, as if to say the state we have is undesirable but one more to their liking is completely acceptable. In this sense I treat them like the aforementioned limited government activists, fellow travelers who have not come to the logical end of their desires.

## Preaching to the Remnant

Albert Jay Nock had written an article in 1936, which appeared in the *Atlantic Monthly,* titled "Isaiah's Job"[40] where he highlighted an Old Testament story of a prophet, and the instructions given to him by his Lord. The story poses there are two types of people, the masses and the remnant, and it is for the remnant not the masses which the preacher should hope to resonate with. As the story goes, the Lord tells Isaiah, and much like Nock I will not vouch for the Lord's word, the remnant, and not the masses will rise up and build a new society when the current society fails. Further it is the purpose of Isaiah to reassure and keep the remnant going. The common misconception about the term masses to mean the impoverished class of proletariat workers is propagated by collectivists and should be rectified here, the masses in reference to this story means simply the majority. The remnant, however is the unknowable, there is no secret society of them, they are camouflaged in plain sight, interdispersed within the masses, getting along the best they can.

The fundamental difference between the masses and the remnant is intellect and character as Nock sees it; he proposes the mass-man as unthinking and unprincipled and

40 http://www.lewrockwell.com/orig3/nock3b.html

the remnant his polar opposite, as Nock puts it "The line of differentiation between the masses and the Remnant is set invariably by quality, not by circumstance."[41] So, in a view common between Nock and myself, the effort should not be towards creating a mass movement, it should be kept to the highest order of integrity, to not dilute the doctrine into a mere placebo.

The mass messenger has fame and fortune in his future; he makes concessions and compromises to appeal to the masses, but thinks not what this does to his doctrine. Certainly there will be applause and recognition but it is at the cost of the message's purity, its meaning, to the point where there is nothing of substance left. The mass man only takes in ideas that are no risk, which are mutable and do not impose him to retain some form of integrity to keep honest about supporting the idea. It is little more than begging that a mass messenger does as he corrupts his message for mass approval. Current days we could call such a mass messenger a sellout, whose chicanery is all too common among the intelligentsia and the state officials of elected office. We see real examples of these mass messengers, calling out promises on soap boxes in order to gain office, and they do meet a wide stature of success in a system that caters to the mass man.

---

41 http://www.lewrockwell.com/orig3/nock3b.html II

He who sends his message out in purity, he who retains the integrity of the message never can claim to be a mass messenger, his message does not conform to mass will.  He does not resonate with the mass man mainly because he calls out the shame of the mass man, the mass man's nature of ignorance and complacency.  The messenger to the remnant meets no lavish success, has no means to gain mass approval, is shunned as a radical or more often insane, and does not gain heavily in the body politic.  The reward for such a purpose is within, though there is little fame or fortune to being a messenger to the remnant it is an interesting job, as Nock states:

"What chiefly makes it so, I think, is that in any given society the Remnant are always so largely an unknown quantity. You do not know, and will never know, more than two things about them. You can be sure of those – dead sure, as our phrase is – but you will never be able to make even a respectable guess at anything else. You do not know, and will never know, who the Remnant are, nor what they are doing or will do. Two things you do know, and no more: First, that they exist; second, that they will find you. Except for these two certainties, working for the Remnant means working in impenetrable darkness; and this, I should say, is just the condition calculated most effectively to pique the interest of any prophet who is properly gifted with the imagination, insight and intellectual curiosity necessary to a successful pursuit of his trade."[42]

## Strategy

I see there is no way to truly change the "hearts and minds" of the masses, it is an effort in futility as the heart and mind of the masses is easily led astray; you never truly change them because they never truly have a shape to change in the first place. It is the remnant who will understand the principled integrity of a pure message; they will adhere to it and spread it among themselves. Education and agorism will resonate with the remnant, some may attend to the ballot for a candidate and a scant few could be led to revolt.

The message of liberty, I am almost certain, will never resonate with the mass man, it requires him to think and accept responsibility, two traits which are as alien to the mass man as breathing chlorine gas, I would wager as fatal as well. The mass man will fall under the banner of another tyrant in violence or heed the duplicitous promises of their prime sycophants, i.e. the politician and the intelligentsia, who will in the former lead them in death and the latter in slavery. Liberty will only be appreciated by the remnant, they are the only portion of society which has

---

42 http://www.lewrockwell.com/orig3/nock3b.html IV

the depth of character to not only understand it, but also live by it.

It was not my purpose on the onset of this book to change anyone's mind, just show that minds can change...

# Acknowledgements

I offer these acknowledgments to the many people responsible for the formulation and cultivation of these ideas in my head; they are by no means in any order:

Diana Culda
Ken Abate
Maggie Shai Terry and her husband Cody
Dan Browe
Mike Deen
Jeremy Deen
Mary Ann Bowling
Jason Cummins
Carl Cline
Roger Pooling
Anita Calbert
Jim Davidson

James Cox
Nathaniel Foote
Dan Green

## Of Sodahead
Jason Feffer, creator of Sodahead
Brady969
The Bantam Seditioner
9$^{th}$ of 9
Rastus
And many others of the Sodahead community.

## The Mises Community
Liberty Student
The Laughing Man
Nir Graham
Again, there are many others.

## Those I cannot meet
Ayn Rand
Lysander Spooner
Murray N. Rothbard
Ludwig von Mises and his intellectual predecessors
Albert Jay Nock
Rose Wilder Lane
Thomas Paine
Thomas Jefferson
Patrick Henry
F.A. Hayek
Benjamin Tucker
Etienne de la Boetie
Seneca

Aristotle
And many more...

## The Austrians and Others
Llewellyn H. Rockwell
Dr. Walter Block
Stefan Molyneux
Thomas E. Woods Jr.
Jörg Guido Hülsmann
Roderick T. Long
Robert Murphy
Doug French
Stephan Kinsella
Ron Paul
Miguel Riuz

Without these men and women, many more whom have to remain unsaid, I may not have traversed this journey or if I did it may have taken a far greater time or worse could have taken a far different end. I offer great thanks to all who have in the course of their lives enriched mine in their own way, some who I can never meet, some who I still may and those I have. I cherish the great works I have read, only overshadowed by the great relationships I have formed in the course of these essays. My only hope is to continue to write as I evolve in order to chronicle my experiences as well as cast some insight on the implications thereof, and in doing so reflecting positively on my intellectual predecessors.